THE
WHISTLING
WHIRLIGIG

Other Books by Ben Shecter

SOMEPLACE ELSE

GAME FOR DEMONS

THE
WHISTLING
WHIRLIGIG

by BEN SHECTER

J
She

Harper & Row, Publishers
New York, Evanston, San Francisco, London

THE WHISTLING WHIRLIGIG

Copyright © 1974 by Ben Shecter

Library of Congress Catalog Card Number: 73–5493
Trade Standard Book Number: 06–025591–9
Harpercrest Standard Book Number: 06–025592–7

FIRST EDITION
24278

For
Stephen Sondheim

THE
WHISTLING
WHIRLIGIG

1

"Watch out for Greenleaf's ghost!" the boys shouted, running past Josh's room to the buses. Being left behind was bad enough, Josh thought, without their reminding him of that ghost story. So he pretended not to hear, and at last the buses pulled away, leaving only an echo of the shouting. Josh sat at his desk alone in the empty dormitory, and without realizing it, began drawing ghosts in his notebook.

He had heard about the ghost since he had first entered the Academy. It was an easy story to believe, because Cragsmoor Military Academy looked like an old fortress. It sat on a high hill overlooking the Hudson River, and with its dark drafty corridors it seemed a good place for ghosts.

The ghost was supposed to be Fillmore Green-leaf, the first commandant of the Academy. His head had been blown off, the story went, by a student who had fired a cannon at him. Josh thought that if the first commandant had been any-thing like the present one, he could believe that it had happened. Because Minton Almstead, who headed the Academy now, was awful. The Academy itself was awful. The only thing Josh liked about Cragsmoor was the location. Josh was a good artist and he spent lots of time looking at the river and doing paintings of it.

His parents were divorced, and their last joint decision had been to send him to Cragsmoor. When he protested, they said, "It's for your own good." But Josh knew it was to get him out of their way. He received letters from his mother and phone calls from his father. Just before Thanksgiving vacation his mother wrote him. She was off to Barbados for a rest, she said, and closed the letter by saying she was sorry they couldn't be together at Thanksgiving but she would see him at Christmas.

His father called that week too. He told Josh that his new wife, who was pregnant, wasn't up to

4

having any company. Josh was hurt that his father should think of him as company. Company meant people who just visited. You put on your best behavior for them and you never told them secrets or how you really felt.

Josh thought about his mother and father and the times they had all shared together. It made the present even lonelier. Josh wouldn't even have minded an invitation home from his roommate, Miles Carpenter. But they weren't good friends, and Miles had invited someone else.

So Josh accepted the invitation to have Thanksgiving dinner with Otis Wicker, his history teacher. He knew Josh was alone, and it was kind of him to ask. But it didn't seem right to Josh. Thanksgiving was a family time and Josh would be spending it with a stranger. Otis Wicker was old. He had a leather-gloved artificial hand that made a hard sound when it rested on the desk. Josh thought it must be made of iron.

Josh decided to walk down to the river's edge. A cold November wind turned the leaves, and he burrowed his hands deep into his pockets. The first star came out and Josh wanted to wish on it. But he knew wishing his mother and father together again was wasting a wish, and he didn't wish at all.

The water made a slapping sound as it brushed against the stony shoreline. Josh thought of hiding on a ship and going far away. He looked at the water and wondered how deep and cold it was. He shivered and turned back.

Thanksgiving was a cold day. Josh was happy he didn't have to wear his gray uniform, which he hated. It itched, and he hated it.

Otis Wicker had drawn a map to his house. Josh bicycled there. His nose and ears grew cold quickly. He pretended he was a courier on a secret mission, pursued by enemy agents. He raced along trying not to think about the cold.

The house was at the edge of a small village not far from Cragsmoor. A road wove through the village, with a church, a general store, and a one-room schoolhouse set at the turns. A honey-colored dog followed Josh through the village to the Wicker house.

Otis Wicker's place looked as if it had been put together by gnomes. Old Mr. Wicker looked like a gnome himself.

The house had crooked chimneys and windows. It was set against a hill; a wooden shed and a stone smokehouse that burrowed into the hill hugged each side of it. A deep muddy ditch in front with a bridge over it was all that remained of what had once been a canal. It was the kind of place Josh wanted to draw.

"Hello!" shouted Otis Wicker. He came out of the shed carrying kindling wood.

Josh ran to help him. Although Otis Wicker was sprightly for his age, he seemed relieved to share his load with Josh. His cheeks were red patches, and when he smiled his eyes disappeared under white caterpillar brows. "I see you and Oliver have discovered each other," he said, motioning to the dog, who was now sitting next to the bicycle.

"He followed me all through the village to your house," said Josh.

"That's Oliver, searching for a friend," said Otis Wicker. "He was named after the orphan Oliver Twist. He just appeared in the village one day, and he's never left."

"Who takes care of him?" Josh asked, suddenly feeling sorry for the dog.

"He depends upon the kindness of the villagers. He eats and sleeps where he can."

Josh wanted to ask Mr. Wicker if he could bring

Oliver into the house, but he was afraid it would be rude since he was only a guest himself.

Otis Wicker pushed the front door open with his shoulder and Josh followed him inside. It was warm and friendly. The smell of bread baking and turkey roasting filled the house. A Siamese cat, curled up in a big wing chair, yawned and greeted them.

"That's Daphne," said Mr. Wicker. He placed the kindling wood near the fireplace. Josh did the same with his. "Daphne and Oliver don't get along," said Mr. Wicker. "I've tried, but Daphne gets jealous. And since she was here first it's her house."

Josh disliked the cat. With her Siamese-accented yowl she seemed to be scolding Otis Wicker for Josh's being there.

"Siamese cats are very possessive," said Mr. Wicker, as though he knew what Josh was thinking. "And they're great at keeping secrets." Otis Wicker smiled and winked at the cat.

Josh wondered what he meant, but he figured Mr. Wicker was pretty old and old people act strangely. He remembered when his grandmother had hidden eggs under her pillow.

A fire crackled loudly in the fireplace. A large clock on the mantel chimed.

Mr. Wicker sat in the big wing chair and folded his hands across his stomach. Josh tried to avoid looking at the hand with the leather glove. And the more he didn't want to look at it, the harder it was for him not to. In the classroom Otis Wicker always wore a jacket which concealed it more than the flannel shirt he was now wearing. An uncomfortable silence swelled.

As if aware of Josh's growing discomfort, Otis Wicker got up from his chair and said, "Perhaps we should have our cider."

"Good idea," said Josh, who was beginning to regret being there. He told himself that he would have preferred a bologna sandwich in his room. He sat down by the fire and added, aloud, "You sure have a lot of old stuff."

"I've been collecting antiques for years," said Otis Wicker.

Josh thought the furniture and Mr. Wicker suited each other.

He followed Otis Wicker into the dining room, where a table was elaborately set. There were candles in silver candlesticks, china dishes with golden bands, and crystal glasses that sparkled. Josh knew that Otis Wicker had gone to great trouble preparing the dinner, and he told himself that he was going to make the best of it.

Otis Wicker poured some apple cider into Josh's glass. He filled his own, his eyes twinkling in the candlelight. "There's a place for Daphne," he said.

Daphne soon appeared at the table. Otis Wicker raised his glass. "To secrets," he said.

Josh raised his glass and sipped the cider. It tasted warm and sweet. "To secrets?" he whispered.

2

Lights went on behind frosted windows. Josh bicycled his way back through the village. The cold night air pinched at his face, but Josh felt warm. The dinner at Mr. Wicker's had been a good one. Josh had had second helpings of everything, and Otis Wicker had also given him a bag of food to take back.

When Josh passed the church, Oliver, who had been sitting on the steps, greeted him. "How about some Thanksgiving dinner?" said Josh, getting off his bicycle. The dog jumped up on Josh, knocking him to the ground. He gave Josh's face a good washing.

"I'm not dinner. It's in the bag," laughed Josh. He got to his feet and fed the hungry dog.

Oliver began to follow Josh out of the village toward Cragsmoor. Josh looked into the dog's large almond-shaped eyes. "Listen, Oliver, I'd like to take you with me, but I'm afraid there's no place for you at Cragsmoor. And anyway, you'd hate it there—the uniforms itch, the food is awful, and the guys are always teasing."

At Cragsmoor, Josh spent the rest of the holiday preparing for an algebra exam and listening for strange noises. Withered vines brushing against windows sounded like hushed footsteps. Josh was happy when the first group of boys returned.

Miles Carpenter, Josh's roommate, ran into the room. "See any ghosts?" he shouted, throwing himself on top of his bed.

"Yes," said Josh. "On your bed."

Miles jumped up. "I thought it felt kind of clammy," he laughed. "It takes a lot to scare me," he said boastfully.

Josh had often wished he could really frighten Miles and put an end to his boasting about how fearless he was.

Classes began again and the boys were restless. They talked about their holiday, and some were even making Christmas vacation plans. Josh listened and wondered where he'd be spending Christmas.

The algebra exam had been difficult, and Josh was happy when it was over. He found himself looking forward to history class and seeing old Mr. Wicker again. He thought about the good dinner, and about Otis Wicker's strange toast to secrets. Josh didn't know if Mr. Wicker really meant something by it, or if it was just the ramblings of an old man.

Mr. Wicker wasn't at his desk when Josh entered the room. And when he didn't appear at the start of the class the boys began to horse around. One of the boys pretended he was Otis Wicker with an artificial hand. Everyone laughed. Josh felt uncomfortable, and sorry for Mr. Wicker. The joking came to an abrupt end when Mr. Ivers, the gym instructor, walked into the room. He told the class that Otis Wicker was out ill, and he would substitute for him until he returned.

"There'll be no horsing around when I'm here," said Mr. Ivers, who was a big mean-looking man. All the boys were afraid of him, and they listened when he spoke. It wasn't that way with Otis Wicker. Josh began to worry about old Mr. Wicker, and by the time class was over he had decided to pay him a visit.

After classes, groups of boys gathered on the campus to play touch football. Some of the boys tried to get Josh to join in, but he didn't. He hurried to get his bicycle. The bicycles were stored in the dormitory basement. There Josh ran into Miles Carpenter.

Miles was tinkering with a slide projector, and when he saw Josh he tried to hide it. Josh wondered what Miles was doing, but he didn't ask him.

"Where are you going?" Miles asked Josh.

"Oh, just out for a ride," said Josh.

"Better be back for attendance check," said Miles. "You don't want to get caught by Barton Forbes."

Barton Forbes was the class platoon leader. He did everything by the rules. Inspections, drills, and parades were important to him. Most of the boys didn't like him. Josh was convinced that his main goal in life was to head up all the armed forces of the United States.

"Barton Forbes—that creep doesn't bother me," said Josh, trying to sound as if he didn't care. But he did.

Josh pretended he was making a prison getaway

when he rode past the high stone posts marking the entranceway to Cragsmoor. As he raced along, iced brown leaves made crunching noises as they fragmented beneath the bicycle wheels.

After a sharp bend in the road the village appeared. A stillness hovered over the village as if all sound had been swept away. To Josh it seemed like a place that existed in its own time zone. He suddenly wanted to turn back, but the quiet was broken by a friendly greeting from Oliver.

"Hi, Oliver!" Josh shouted, happy to see him. Barking and wagging his tail, Oliver escorted Josh to Mr. Wicker's front door. "Shh," said Josh, getting off of his bicycle. "Old Mr. Wicker is sick." Oliver stopped barking; he sat down, cocked his head, and looked at Josh quizzically.

Josh knocked on the front door. A crow that lived in the eaves of the smokehouse stuck its head out and eyed Josh suspiciously. He knocked on the door again, and when there wasn't any answer, Josh tapped on the window and pressed his face up against it, calling out, "Mr. Wicker, it's me— Josh!"

"Hello there," said Mr. Wicker, coming up from behind Josh.

Josh jumped. He was startled by Otis Wicker.

He was also surprised to see Mr. Wicker outdoors and looking perfectly healthy. A bag of wild birdseed was resting on his shoulders.

"I—I thought you were sick," said Josh, unable to hide his bewilderment at seeing Otis Wicker looking so fit. "That's what Mr. Ivers said."

"Of course, of course, that's what I told them," said Mr. Wicker, scattering some seeds around. The crow flew down to a low-hanging branch and looked at the seeds. "That's my neighbor and friend."

The crow cawed and Mr. Wicker fed the bird from the palm of his hand. Contented, the bird flew back to the smokehouse and disappeared under the eaves.

Mr. Wicker put down the bag of seed, and a serious expression came across his face. "There's a crisis," he said, looking directly at Josh.

"A crisis?" said Josh.

"Yes," said Mr. Wicker. "Come inside and I'll tell you about it."

Josh wondered about Mr. Wicker with talk about secrets and a crisis. He wanted to tell the old man he was glad he was well, and then get on his bicycle and return to Cragsmoor. But Otis Wicker already had the front door open. He smiled, and extended his arm in a welcoming gesture. Josh felt compelled to go into the house.

Inside the house, Daphne the cat was on the windowsill watching a fly struggle in a web. A table was set in front of the fireplace. On it were a plate full of cookies and two cups.

"You look like you're expecting company," said Josh when he saw the table. "I don't want to interrupt anything."

Mr. Wicker looked at the table and then at Josh. "Oh, no, that's for us," he said.

"For us?" said Josh.

"Yes, I've been expecting you," said Otis Wicker.

Josh looked at the old man strangely.

"Sit down, sit down. I'll get the hot chocolate."

Josh sat down, and an uneasy feeling came over him. Daphne jumped at the fly and it disappeared in her mouth. Josh cringed, imagining what the fly must taste like.

"Were you expecting me too?" Josh said, looking at the cat.

Daphne closed her eyes, and Josh was positive she smiled.

3

The awful feeling of being trapped by a wrong decision took hold of Josh. Confused and eager to get back to Cragsmoor before attendance check, he tapped a spoon nervously on a cup. He waited impatiently for Otis Wicker to reappear. Each time he looked at the mantel clock the hands seemed to be in the very same place.

When Otis Wicker did come back he acted like a concerned innkeeper.

"My very special blend of hot chocolate," he said. "It's made from the finest African cocoa beans." He poured the chocolate and then topped it off with a large serving of whipped cream.

"It looks delicious," said Josh, wanting to finish

in a hurry and then leave. He drank the chocolate and burned the roof of his mouth.

"I must warn you, it's very hot. Be careful," said Mr. Wicker.

"It's too late!" Josh said to himself. He touched the spot with his tongue, knowing there would soon be a blister there.

Josh was beginning to think Mr. Wicker's talk of crisis was something he had made up, because he didn't look troubled as he sipped his hot chocolate.

"Have a cookie," said Otis Wicker, lifting the plate. "I baked them myself."

Biting into the cookie was painful for Josh— it seemed to scratch the burn.

"Something wrong?" asked Mr. Wicker, noticing the expression on Josh's face.

Josh shook his head No. But he told himself Yes—everything was wrong.

The plate of cookies went crashing to the floor when Mr. Wicker accidently turned it over with his artificial hand. Josh looked at the hand, and then quickly got to his knees and picked up the cookies and plate.

Otis Wicker caught Josh's eye and bent his right

arm at the elbow. The hand remained motionless. "It's wooden," he said, tapping the palm of it with the index finger of his left hand.

Not knowing how to react, Josh whispered, "I'm sorry."

"Oh, it happened when I was a youngster on the farm, feeding my father's threshing machine. I could have this wooden hand replaced by one of those mechanical things, but it has served me well for so long now, I just keep it." He said it matter-of-factly, like a story told many times before.

Terrible images came to Josh, and he suddenly imagined his hands being caught in such a machine. And then trying to draw pictures with mechanical hands.

The image grew uncomfortably strong in Josh's mind, and, wanting to erase it immediately, he changed the subject.

"You said something before about a crisis."

An expression of gloom came to Mr. Wicker's face. "I don't want to ruin a perfectly good hot chocolate by discussing it now," said Mr. Wicker.

He filled a plate full of whipped cream and fed it to the cat. She licked it up quickly and the loudest sound in the room was her purring.

20

"Now that's what I call a happy cat," said Mr. Wicker, taking Daphne in his arms.

"I'm glad *she's* happy," Josh mumbled to himself.

"I'm sorry, I didn't hear you. What did you say, Josh?"

"I said she sure looks happy." The chocolate cooled and Josh drank it once again.

Mr. Wicker's face rested against the cat's, and looking at them from over the rim of his cup Josh thought they formed one strange-looking creature. The question of how Mr. Wicker knew beforehand of his visit began to gnaw at Josh.

Finally he said very directly, "Mr. Wicker, how did you know I was going to be here today?"

"It's a gift." The old man smiled, putting the cat down.

"What kind of gift?" asked Josh.

"I'll tell you about it sometime. Shall I tell you about my crisis?"

Otis Wicker had Josh so bewildered that he wanted to say, "No, I don't want to hear about your crisis, and if I don't leave soon I'll have one of my own." But he remained seated and watched the old man get up from the table and go to a slant-topped desk. It was a large desk, and when Mr. Wicker opened the top, papers spilled out onto the floor.

"Now where is it?" Mr. Wicker whispered to himself. He turned on a lamp with a green glass shade. Shadows stretched across the room. And Mr. Wicker's hair and brows took on the green color from the lamp, making him look even more like an old gnome. He searched frantically through the papers until he came to one that he held high above his head. "Here's the rotten thing!" he shouted.

He returned to the table and looked directly at Josh. "I suppose you've heard about the airport they are planning to build near here?"

"No I haven't, sir," said Josh.

"Well, they are," said Mr. Wicker. A trace of anger touched his voice. "I just received this letter today," he said. "It's from the state highway commission." Mr. Wicker read the letter to himself, mumbling some words out loud. His face grew red. "Do you know what they want to do? They want to tear down this house to make way for a road!"

Josh looked around the room. It was a friendly

place with its wide ceiling beams, large fireplace, and crooked windows.

"I'll not move," said Mr. Wicker, pounding his hand on the table. "We can't move," he whispered to Daphne.

Josh found himself feeling sorry for the fate of the house rather than that of Mr. Wicker. The burning log in the fireplace split, sending a shower of sparks up to the smoke-stained mantel. Suddenly Josh said, "They can't do that. It's a forever house."

Mr. Wicker seemed startled and he leaned forward. "What did you say?"

"I said it's a forever house. I mean like it's been here so long, it wouldn't be right for it not to be here anymore."

"That's exactly how I feel about it," said Mr. Wicker. "I'm glad you feel that way—it will make things easier."

"Easier for what?" asked Josh.

"O-o-o-hhh uh mmmnn—" Otis Wicker seemed genuinely flustered by the question. He regained his composure and said, "I might need your help in the future."

"My help?" said Josh.

23

"Yes," said the old man, standing at the fire-place with his back toward Josh.

"How can I help?" said Josh.

"Oh, I'm sure the occasion will arise when I need your help." The flickering firelight made his dwarflike shape take on an animated spirit.

Josh wondered what kind of help he could be to Mr. Wicker.

4

Mr. Wicker waved good-bye from the front door. A lantern on the bridge washed the house in a dim copper glow. Josh looked back and couldn't imagine the house not being there. It was a part of the hill, and of the village. Without it things wouldn't be right.

The chapel bells of Cragsmoor tolled and the neighboring villagers knew it was six o'clock. Josh ran up the dormitory steps, keeping his fingers crossed, hoping that Barton Forbes hadn't gotten to his room yet for attendance check. He rushed in just as the platoon leader arrived with his clipboard.

"You look out of breath, Newman," said Barton Forbes, giving Josh a long hard look.

"I was just in the bathroom," said Josh.

"It's a bad place to be around attendance check time," he said.

"I know," said Josh, "but I couldn't help it."

Barton Forbes told them that there was going to be an inspection that weekend and that they'd better shape up.

Miles Carpenter had been to the library; his desk was cluttered with books. One was open to a picture of a Civil War officer. When he saw Josh looking at it, he closed the book. He also put away some camera equipment that was on his footlocker.

Josh knew Miles was up to something, but he couldn't figure out what it was. And he knew asking him would be dumb, because if Miles wanted him to know, he would tell him.

The mess hall at dinnertime was noisy, and some of the boys were having fun passing trays to each other. Mr. Ivers appeared at the doorway and the noise faded. The only sound in the mess hall was that of the utensils.

Miles whispered to Josh, "You were almost late for attendance check. Where were you?"

Josh ignored the question and bit into a hard roll. He sighed in pain because of the blister in his mouth.

Mr. Wicker appeared in class the next day. And he winked at Josh. The class lesson was about the Underground Railway in the North. Mr. Wicker explained how the very area they were in was a center for runaway slaves.

Otis Wicker spoke as if he had almost been there and experienced it himself. Vivid pictures of black people escaping and hiding filled Josh's head.

After class Mr. Wicker called Josh aside and told him not to mention the crisis to anyone. Josh told him that he had his word. But Josh really couldn't understand why.

At mail call that day Josh knew there was a letter for him. Among the letters Barton Forbes was holding Josh could see the familiar pink envelope his mother always used. Barton Forbes knew who the letter was for, and before giving it to Josh he passed it under his nose and sniffed it. Her stationery was lilac-scented, and sometimes when he was alone Josh would smell it, trying to remember his mother, whom he hadn't seen in a long time.

His mother started the letter out with the usual "How are you? I miss you." Then she went on to tell Josh about a group of people she had met in Barbados and how they had invited her to Palm Beach for Christmas. Although she had told them

No, if she did change her mind, she knew Josh would understand.

Josh crumpled up the letter. He knew now he wouldn't be seeing his mother at Christmas.

Before dinner the next evening, Josh got a phone call from his father. He told Josh that he would be up to see him Sunday and they would have lunch together. The call made Josh happy, and he eagerly awaited his father's visit.

He worked hard preparing for the coming inspection. Even though he told himself it was a dumb thing, he wanted to pass it so he wouldn't end up with any restrictions.

In preparing for the inspection, Miles Carpenter removed some camera equipment and a slide projector from his footlocker and placed them in a box, and put that in his closet.

Unable to hold back his curiosity, Josh said, "Going in for photography?"

"Yeah!" answered Miles and then he asked Josh if he could borrow his shoe polish.

Josh was disappointed, because he knew Miles was up to something.

Barton Forbes went from room to room telling the boys they had better shape up because the

28

commandant was going to be really strict on this inspection.

"If anyone messes up, they'll have to answer to me personally!" he shouted.

Josh felt like punching him in the nose. He was sure most of the boys felt the same way. And knowing that was almost as good as a punch.

On the day of inspection, Josh dressed in his newly pressed uniform and starched shirt. The uniform itched more than ever, and the shirt irritated his neck.

"Cadets, attention!" shouted Barton Forbes. The inspection began. The boys stood rigidly beside their open footlockers. In each locker was a neat display of camping equipment.

Barton Forbes accompanied Commandant Almstead on the inspection. The platoon leader carried his familiar clipboard, recording scores reported to him by the commandant. Everything was inspected, from belt buckles to beds.

When they entered Josh's room, Josh could hear his heart beating loudly, and his hands were moist from perspiration.

Minton Almstead was a tall thin man who walked erect and carried a swagger stick. He called the

boys "men." Josh knew the commandant secretly hoped for a war to break out so that he could lead them all into battle.

As he approached, Josh was able to smell the commandant's brandy-scented cologne. It almost made him dizzy.

The commandant looked Josh up and down. "Newman, haircut!" He pronounced it like a court-room verdict of "Guilty!" Josh grew warm to the tips of his ears. He watched Barton Forbes record the mark against him. Then the platoon leader gave Josh a squinty-eyed I'll-see-you-later look.

When inspection was over, Barton Forbes returned to Josh's room. "We'll find some proper punishment for you," he said.

Josh was determined to ask his father to take him out of Cragsmoor. "Anyplace would be better," he told himself.

5

"How's my little soldier?" was Josh's father's greeting to him.

"Okay," Josh answered, but he wanted to say, "I'm not a little soldier and I don't want to be one."

His father took a puff of his cigar and turned up the collar on his topcoat. "It's cold in these parts; we city folk aren't used to this country air."

Josh knew his father was trying to kid around and break an uncomfortable feeling between them. It was almost as if he were trying to make up for Thanksgiving, or else was about to spring a new surprise upon Josh. Josh hoped his father would say that he was leaving his new wife, and that from now on it was just going to be the two of them.

They walked to the parking lot in silence. Josh

was surprised when he didn't see the blue Chevy he remembered. Instead he followed his father to a white Cadillac Eldorado.

"How do you like it?" his father said proudly.

"It's nice," said Josh, who really didn't pay too much attention to cars. "What happened to the other one?" he asked.

His father looked at him. "Nothing happened to it," he said. "Just thought I'd trade it in for something special."

"Probably bought it for his new wife," thought Josh.

Josh got in the car beside his father. "What do you want to hear?" his father said, handing him a big stack of tapes. "You name it, I've got it—all the new ones too!"

"Makes no difference to me," said Josh.

"Just choose any one," said his father, almost annoyed at Josh's indifference.

Josh put the first tape on the pile into the slot. Some guy wailing about his baby baby came blaring through all parts of the car.

"That's some stereo system!" said his father. "The best money can buy."

All the songs sounded alike; they were all about

"baby baby." Josh entertained himself by looking out of the window. And every time he saw an old house he thought about Mr. Wicker's place, and wondered what was going to happen to it.

"Where do you want to eat?" his father shouted above the music noise.

Josh shrugged his shoulders. It seemed a dumb question, because he wasn't familiar with restaurants in the area.

"We'll find someplace," said his father. Cigar ashes fell on his coat. Josh wanted to see them burn a hole in it, but they didn't, and he was disappointed.

"Hungry?" his father asked.

"I guess so," said Josh.

"I could eat a horse," said his father.

Josh looked at his father and believed he could. They drove past several hamburger places. Josh liked hamburgers a lot, but when he suggested one, his father said, "Nothing doing! When I take you out we eat good!"

"But I like hamburgers," said Josh.

His father laughed and said, "That's junk food! You've got to get some meat on your bones. I mean after all, how are you going to become a general?" His father chuckled to himself.

Josh had the impression that his father thought he was training for an army career at Cragsmoor.

At a bend in the road they came across a large white-columned building. A sign hung between the center columns telling them that it was the Vanderlyn Inn serving lunches and dinners.

"Now that looks like an interesting place," said his father, and he parked the car alongside the building.

They entered the dining room through a dimly lighted center hall. Dusty plastic palms guarded either side of the entranceway.

"We're going into the ining oom," said Josh.

"What?" said his father, looking at him puzzled.

Josh pointed to a neon DINING ROOM sign. The D and R were not glowing.

The only person in the room was an elderly man eating alone at a corner table. He looked up and smiled when Josh and his father walked into the room.

An old lady in a black dress with white collar and cuffs came up from behind them.

"Lunch?" she asked.

"Lunch for two hungry men!" said Josh's father loudly, and he winked at him. Josh felt embarrassed. They were seated in front of a boarded-up fireplace. Someone had painted a tropical scene where the opening had once been.

"Country places like this surprise you," said his father, looking around. "They probably serve terrific home-style cooking."

Josh hoped his father was right because by now he was hungry. He ordered roast chicken with dressing.

"What do you hear from your mother?" his father asked. And before Josh had a chance to answer, his father said, "Never have to worry about her; she knows how to take care of herself."

When the food arrived it was awful. Josh picked at his. "Well, you can't win 'em all," his father said.

Josh forced a smile, and listened to his stomach grumble.

"Pat really wanted to come along," said his father. "But being pregnant and all, she didn't want to take the long trip."

"Oh, that's all right," said Josh. He didn't want to see her anyway, and he was sure she didn't care about seeing him.

Josh looked at his father. He seemed changed. He looked like an old man trying to be young. His hair was combed differently, and his clothing looked like it belonged to a younger person. Josh figured that was what happened when a man his father's age married someone young enough to be his daughter.

"So how are you doing, son?" his father said, chomping down on a fresh cigar.

Josh was about to tell him how he wanted to leave the Academy, but once again his father interrupted. He said, "I'm really proud of you doing well at Cragsmoor." His father looked at him. "You're growing up, Josh. You've changed."

"You've changed too, Daddy," Josh said to himself.

"I might be moving to Arizona," his father said. "I'm going to relocate my business there."

Josh felt a lump in his throat.

"But that won't affect your schooling any. You'll stay right here. Pat and I are going to have a room set aside just for you, when you come to visit." His father laughed. "And you'll have a brother or a sister to play with."

The ride back to Cragsmoor was a silent one. When they got there, his father said, "I almost forgot. I have something for you!" He opened the trunk of the car and handed Josh a box. "It's just a dart game," he said.

As he drove away, he shouted out of the window, "I'll call you soon, and keep up the good work."

Josh waved good-bye. A cold river wind raced across the campus. Tears fell, hurting Josh's face. He whispered, "Daddy, why didn't you take me away from here?"

6

Barton Forbes called a meeting of all the boys who had failed to pass the inspection. "I wonder what kind of punishment he plans," Josh thought. Various kinds of torture treatments came to his mind.

"Attention, cadets!" shouted Barton Forbes. The boys quickly came to attention. "Cadets? You don't even deserve to be called that," shouted the platoon leader. "You're all just little boys who don't know how to take care of yourselves."

While Josh stood there he made up a list of people he hated a lot and Barton Forbes was at the top of it. He also told himself that when he got to be older like Barton Forbes, he would be nice to younger boys.

The platoon leader continued snarling and shouting, and told them to get their camping equipment ready because the next weekend they would be going on an overnight camping trip. He finished by saying, "When I'm through with you you'll be cadets worthy of being here at Cragsmoor."

"Who wants to be a Cragsmoor cadet anyway?" Josh asked himself. He felt like shouting it out.

Most times an overnight camp would be a welcome thing. But Josh knew this trip was going to be unpleasant. It was for punishment, and outdoor living in the wintertime wasn't any fun.

All the boys were dismissed from the formation except those who needed haircuts. Barton Forbes said he would personally escort them to the barber.

The barbershop in town was a one-chair operation and Josh squirmed as he waited his turn. The boys before him were almost bald when the barber finished. Josh wanted to get up and run, but he didn't know where to run to.

Barton Forbes watched, grinning. A pile of hair surrounded the barber's chair, and Josh thought of pouring glue all over the platoon leader and pushing him into the pile. He imagined hunters shooting dead the hairy monster of Cragsmoor.

When Josh left the shop his head felt cold and

naked. He wished he could draw his head inside himself the way a turtle could.

Plotting ways to get rid of Barton Forbes became an important part of Josh's thoughts. But they all ended with Josh picturing himself serving a prison sentence for doing away with the platoon leader.

Gradually Josh's ideas turned to ones of escaping from Cragsmoor. At first the plans were impractical, such as building a raft for a river escape. As the day of the camping trip approached, getting away seemed like a good idea, and different plans came to Josh.

He settled on the idea of bicycling to New York City. There he would change his name and get a job as an apprentice in an art studio.

At night Josh lay awake thinking about the plan and his future. He imagined himself working hard and becoming a famous artist. His mother and father would plead for him to live with them. But he would only agree if they all lived together.

Josh got a map and started to figure out the best possible route to the city. The day before the hike he went to get his bicycle, but it wasn't there. He searched around and began to question some of the boys about its disappearance. No one knew what had happened to it. A feeling of hopelessness came over Josh. He returned to his room and got his camping equipment ready.

It was dark when he was awakened for the hike. He rubbed his eyes and dressed in the cold room. "I hate you, Barton Forbes," he said. His teeth chattered.

Roll call was in front of the dormitory. The pack on Josh's back grew heavy as he listened to the platoon leader shout instructions about the hike.

A piece of gray sky appeared on the other side of the river and began to push away the darkness. By the time they set out, the sky was a rain-promising color. In double file they followed Barton Forbes into the woods that bordered one side of the Academy.

The dim morning light made the trees appear like pastel strokes on wet paper. Soft edges blended into each other. They hiked along a narrow path, ducking and bending away from low-hanging branches and thorny vines. Painful cries were heard each time a twig snapped against a cold face or a thorn took hold and scratched.

After a while the path became a snakelike trail that curled down a rocky ravine. Barton Forbes walked surefootedly, but most of the boys had trouble keeping up the fast pace he set. Josh slipped and took hold of a large tree root; it fragmented at his touch. It was old and rotted. He bruised his knees, but quickly got to his feet because he was afraid of being left behind.

Josh limped along and he wondered what had happened to his bicycle. "If it had only been there," he told himself.

The boys complained of being tired, and Barton Forbes said, "Stop acting like a bunch of sissies and start acting like men!"

Josh wanted to tell him he wasn't a man yet, and that he had different ideas of how men were supposed to act.

One boy was asthmatic; he had trouble breathing and lagged behind. Barton Forbes threatened to leave him there if he didn't keep up with the rest. Josh felt sorry for him and took his pack to help.

A lead-colored sky descended upon the woods, turning it into what seemed like a great stockade. Then rain began to fall, at first gently but soon becoming a heavy downpour.

The boys huddled against the trees, seeking protection, but the wintertime trees gave them little shelter. Barton Forbes gave orders to make camp.

Josh had difficulty setting up his tent. But when he did, he was happy to get out of the steady downfall.

Inside, he listened to the rain. He thought about Mr. Wicker's lesson on the Underground Railway and the runaway slaves, and he wondered if any of them had hidden in that very forest. Josh pictured himself in a similar escape from Barton Forbes. His thoughts were interrupted when one of the boys poked his head into the tent and said, "Orders from Forbes—we're packing up and going back."

It continued raining as they headed back to the Academy. Josh was wet to his skin. When he arrived at Cragsmoor he was tired and cold.

Two days after the hike Josh was in the infirmary with a bad cold. Otis Wicker came to visit. He carried a small package under his arm. Josh was happy to see the old teacher; having a visitor was a nice thing.

"I am sorry you're sick," said Mr. Wicker. "You'd better get well soon. I might be needing your help."

"I'll help you if I can," said Josh.

"I might call on you to look after Daphne for a day or two if I have to go to Albany on matters concerning the house."

"Sure," said Josh. Then he told Mr. Wicker about his missing bicycle.

"Yes, I know," said Mr. Wicker.

Josh looked surprised. "You know?" he said.

"Yes, yes, I heard it from someone," muttered Otis Wicker.

When Mr. Wicker got ready to leave he put his package down on the bedside table. "From Daphne, Oliver, and me," he said and waved good-bye.

Josh thanked him and said "Good-bye." He opened the package. It was a book of ghost stories.

Lying in bed, Josh thought about his illness and imagined himself getting worse. Then he pictured himself dying, and he wondered if his mother and father would come to his funeral.

7

Frost covered the dormitory windows, inside and out. It was a cold Saturday morning. Josh was happy there weren't any drills or inspections that day. He buried himself under his blankets. Miles Carpenter was awake, and he moaned, "Oh, it's freezing in here!"

"If this room doesn't get any warmer I'll be back in the infirmary," said Josh. His teeth chattered.

"I'll be joining you there," said Miles Carpenter. But he jumped out of bed and began to dress. "It will probably be warmer on the soccer field."

Josh watched as Miles pulled his gray and maroon jersey over a sweat shirt. "Time for breakfast," said Miles, and he tugged at Josh's blankets.

"Hey, do you want me to freeze to death?" Josh yelled. He got a hammerlock on Miles and the two of them went wrestling to the floor.

Miles used an after-shave lotion, although he didn't shave. And when Josh kidded him about it, he said, "There's nothing wrong with smelling good, is there?"

Josh had Miles pinned to the floor, and when Miles struggled to free himself Josh could smell the lime-sweet scent of the after-shave. It reminded Josh of summertime, and he liked the smell.

Miles overpowered Josh. Once on top Miles seemed satisfied. He jumped up and threw his soccer shoes over his shoulders and raced down the corridor whistling.

After breakfast Josh returned to his room. The radiators were hissing and the inside window frost had melted. Josh sat at his desk and drew a picture of Barton Forbes. He pinned it to his dart board and took careful aim to get him between the eyes. "You're wiped out, Forbes," shouted Josh as the third dart landed right on target.

Back at his desk Josh drew awhile, and then decided to go for a walk. He went to the soccer field and stayed there watching the game. Then he walked to the river. There was ice on it. A large freighter with a knifelike bow sliced through the river and sent clouds of smoke into the clear winter sky. Josh remained on the riverbank until the ship was part of the horizon.

Mail call was at noon on Saturday. Josh hurried back to the dormitory. There was a letter for him from his mother. Miles was absent from the mail call and Josh accepted a small package for him. From the return address and size, Josh figured it was film slides. He placed the package on Miles' bed, and put his mother's letter unopened under his own pillow.

After lunch, alone in his room, Josh read the letter.

Dearest Josh,

I know we haven't seen each other in a while, but that does not mean I don't care about you. I am always thinking about you, and I miss you terribly. Unfortunately your father put me in a difficult position. I find myself working very hard, and needless to say, Josh, I am tired. You are a bright boy and therefore I'm sure you can understand the decision I've come to about spending the Christmas holidays in Palm Beach. Dear Josh, I find it absolutely necessary to get away and get some rest.

Your Uncle Morton and Aunt Ellen, who love you dearly, said that they would be delighted to have you with them at Christmastime.

Josh didn't finish reading the letter. He crumpled it up and threw it against the dart board. Uncle Morton and Aunt Ellen weren't Josh's favorites. The idea of spending the entire Christmas vacation with them seemed like one of the most awful things that could happen to anyone.

"I don't like them. I won't go!" Josh shouted out loud.

His Uncle Morton was always pretending to be the good guy, but he was really bossy, and when he didn't have his way, Josh knew he could be mean. And his Aunt Ellen was fussy about being neat and clean. She was the only person he knew who would rinse off a bar of soap before using it. They didn't have any children of their own, and Josh figured that if they had one it probably would have turned out to be like Barton Forbes. Josh knew they hated kids.

49

He looked at the pink crumpled letter on the floor. "Mother, why don't you take me with you?" he whispered.

Miles Carpenter rushed into the room, his face red, and his shoes muddied. "Hey," he shouted, "your bicycle is back."

Josh looked at him in disbelief. Miles extended his arms outward, and with a pair of shoes around his neck, he looked like a peddler. "Honest," he said. "Go down and see for yourself."

Miles reached for the package on his bed. Josh said, "I picked it up for you at mail call," and he ran out the door.

The bicycle was there as Miles had said it was. Josh went back to his room to dress for a ride. "I wonder where it was," he said.

Miles shrugged his shoulders. "Maybe someone borrowed it?"

Without any planned destination Josh got on his bicycle. After riding awhile he found himself headed toward Otis Wicker's house. As he rode through the village he was disappointed when he wasn't greeted by Oliver. He had also expected Mr. Wicker to be in front of his house, and when he wasn't there an uneasy feeling of being at a strange place came to Josh.

The feeling went away when Mr. Wicker appeared at his door and waved to Josh. The crow left his smokehouse nest to greet Josh on the bridge railing. The crow seemed friendly, but when Josh wanted to touch him, he hopped to the other side of the bridge.

"He's a cautious fellow," said Mr. Wicker. The crow cawed and flew up to the smokehouse roof, perching himself on a crooked little cupola. He fluttered his wings up and down.

"If he had a propeller on his beak he'd look like a whirligig."

"What's a whirligig?" asked Josh, thinking it was a word Mr. Wicker had just made up.

A thoughtful expression came into Otis Wicker's eyes. "Hmn." He rubbed his chin. "A whirligig is sort of a wind toy. They're used in places where some people would place weathervanes—they're rooftop objects," said Mr. Wicker. "The wind sets them in motion. Some whirligigs are merely figures with paddle arms that go around, and others are more complicated. I've seen a propeller-designed one that sets off two figures sawing a piece of wood."

"What are they made out of?" asked Josh, fascinated by the idea of a wind toy, thinking he would like to make one.

"They are usually made of wood or tin, sometimes both." Mr. Wicker looked at Josh. "Planning on making one?"

"Might be fun," said Josh.

"I'd be glad to help you," said Mr. Wicker. He invited Josh into the house.

"I got my bicycle back," said Josh.

"So I noticed," said Otis Wicker, and he closed the door behind him.

Josh was almost expecting to find some hot chocolate waiting for him. Instead he saw that Mr. Wicker had been working at his desk. Daphne greeted Josh with a rub against his leg.

"I suppose she is beginning to know me," said Josh. He gently stroked the cat.

"I've been busy letter writing," said Mr. Wicker, looking hopelessly at the clutter on his desk. "I'm writing to the governor about saving this house. A trip to Albany might even be necessary."

Mr. Wicker seemed weary. "It's going to be a struggle." He held the letter and then put it down again.

"You'll win," said Josh, wanting to cheer him up.

"This might be my last Christmas in this house," said Mr. Wicker, looking around the room. And then he looked at Josh. "I suppose you'll be going home for Christmas?" he said.

Josh felt like crying. He shook his head No. Then he told Mr. Wicker about the letter he had received that day, and he told him all about his aunt and uncle.

"They hate kids. They really do," he said.

Mr. Wicker listened and pulled at his ear.

When Josh finished speaking, Mr. Wicker got up and said, "How about some chocolate?"

"Sure," said Josh. He was really disappointed. He had hoped Mr. Wicker would say, "How terrible," or "Poor Josh!" Perhaps he wasn't listening at all?

Mr. Wicker went into the kitchen and in a short time he called Josh in. Josh had never been in the kitchen and he was surprised to see a fireplace there too. Herbs, pots, and pans hung from ceiling beams. Spice jars crowded wall shelves. Otis Wicker hovered over a kettle steaming on the huge black stove.

Mr. Wicker turned to Josh. His glasses were all steamy and he looked over them when he spoke.

"I have an idea," he said. "What if I wrote a letter to your mother and told her I would be your guardian during the Christmas holidays? I would tell her you were helping me with a special project. If it works out, you can avoid your aunt and uncle, and spend Christmas with Daphne and me."

Josh smiled. "I'd like that," he said.

After the hot chocolate, Josh and Mr. Wicker wrote a letter to his mother. "I wonder if she will agree," said Josh.

"I hope so," said Mr. Wicker. He crossed his fingers and held them up. Josh crossed his too.

Mr. Wicker served another cup of chocolate and he brought out a platter of cream puffs.

Mr. Wicker's endless supply of goodies delighted Josh. And Mr. Wicker himself seemed to take great joy in surprises.

The cream puffs were the best Josh had ever eaten. He told himself that it wasn't polite to take a third one, but he did. He looked around the kitchen. It was a spice-scented room with shadowed corners and many cupboards. Josh thought it looked like a room with secret places. "Any ghosts in this house?" asked Josh jokingly.

Mr. Wicker bit down hard on a pastry and the cream exploded onto his face. "What did you say?" he asked, wiping his chin.

It was difficult for Josh not to laugh. "I wondered

if there were any ghosts in this house," said Josh. "It seems like a good place for one."

Mr. Wicker spoke in almost a whisper. "I'm sure this house has its share of secrets. It has been here a long time. Many people were born and died here." Mr. Wicker looked at Josh and then continued. "Do you like ghost stories?" he asked.

"Sure," said Josh.

Mr. Wicker smiled. "So do I." He ate another cream puff and said, "One day I'll tell you one I know."

Josh wasn't sure he wanted to hear one in that kitchen. He thanked Mr. Wicker for the treats and left.

Outside Oliver was waiting near the bicycle. Josh was happy he was there, and he gave the dog a big hug.

8

"God rest ye merry, gentlemen . . ." The glee-club voices rang out across the campus. They were practicing in the chapel for the Christmas concert.

Josh left the crafts room carrying the crow whirligig he was making for Mr. Wicker. He thought it would be a nice gift for him. As he passed the chapel he pretended he was a part of the glee club and he joined in singing the Christmas carol. He continued singing until he got to the dormitory. Josh wished he had the musical ability to be a member, but he knew he would always be a listener.

The boy across the hall rushed past Josh on the stairway. He shouted excitedly, "Hey, my parents just called. They're taking me to Acapulco for the holidays."

"That's great," said Josh. It wasn't the trip to Mexico that Josh envied. It was the fact that this boy was going to be with his mother and father for Christmas.

Josh's mother hadn't replied to Mr. Wicker's letter. Josh really hoped she would change her mind about going away, and they would be together for Christmas.

There was a party mood at Cragsmoor, and Josh felt like the new kid on the street who wasn't invited. An unhappiness enveloped Josh, and he tried to convince himself that Christmas was just for little kids, nothing more than a date on a calendar.

"What's that?" shouted Miles Carpenter when Josh walked into the room.

"What's what?" asked Josh.

"That thing under your arm," said Miles, pointing.

Josh had almost forgotten what he was carrying. "It's going to be a whirligig," he said.

"A what?" shouted Miles.

"A whirligig, it's kind of a wind toy," explained Josh.

"Sounds like a ride in an amusement park," said Miles.

"It does," smiled Josh, and he put it away.

Miles Carpenter walked around the room with his hockey skates on.

"Do you know what I'm going to do all Christmas?" he asked.

Josh shrugged his shoulders.

"I'm going to play hockey on the pond near my house, that's what I'm going to do," said Miles.

"Sounds like fun," said Josh without any real enthusiasm in his voice.

"Going to spend Christmas with your father?" Miles asked.

"No," said Josh. "He's going to be in Arizona."

"Oh, then you'll be with your mother," said Miles.

Josh shook his head No. "I'm going to be with my aunt and uncle. They've invited me. They don't have any kids and at Christmastime they like to have one around. So my mother thought it would be a good idea if I were with them." Josh felt funny lying about something as dumb as his Christmas vacation, but he found it difficult to tell Miles the truth.

Miles looked at Josh and Josh turned away. He felt his eyes getting watery. He took a deep breath and forced a smile. "Boy, everyone's going crazy around here and there's still four more days before Christmas vacation begins."

"It's getting away from this place that's really great!" said Miles.

"I suppose that's the important thing," said Josh, half to himself.

It was difficult for Josh to pay attention to any classwork. He could think of nothing but hearing from his mother, and the waiting seemed endless. He was beginning to give up all hope.

He was almost afraid to open it when he finally did receive a letter from her. His heart raced and he crossed his fingers.

She told him although it was against her better judgment she agreed to go along with his plan. She also told Josh how disappointed his aunt and uncle were.

"I'll bet," said Josh when he came to that part. "I'm sure they didn't have to have their arms twisted to give me up for Christmas. They're probably celebrating," he told himself. "Well, so am I!"

Josh felt let down that his mother hadn't changed her mind about spending Christmas with him. But he consoled himself with the fact that he didn't have to be with his mean Uncle Morton and his fussy Aunt Ellen. Eager to tell Mr. Wicker the news, Josh headed for his house.

Mr. Wicker was delighted and he insisted upon showing Josh the room that was going to be his for the holidays. Up until that moment it hadn't occurred to Josh that he would be staying at Mr. Wicker's house. And now that it was going to happen he had mixed feelings about the idea.

Josh followed Mr. Wicker up a narrow winding stairway that had been hidden behind a wide planked door. The upstairs of the house had low angled ceilings that were fine for someone Josh's size, but anyone taller would have to duck and bend at each turn. Even Mr. Wicker, who was not much taller than Josh, had to stoop.

He opened the door to a small room, most of which was taken up with a four-poster bed that stood in the middle of it. The walls were yellow, and stenciled with bluebirds and thistles.

"This will be your room," said Mr. Wicker.

Josh liked the four-poster bed. He had never slept in one before. He liked the room, too, because the birds on the walls made it seem like a happy place.

"It's a nice room," said Josh. He felt like jumping up and down on the bed. It seemed perfect for it.

Back at Cragsmoor Josh found himself almost looking forward to spending Christmas at Mr. Wicker's. He received a check in the mail from his father as his Christmas present. There was also a card signed "Dad and Pat," which Josh quickly tore up.

The glee club gave its Christmas concert and Josh liked listening to their carols. Only good things were sung about in Christmas songs. They made Josh picture olden times with gentle people having fun.

Josh finished his whirligig. It looked like the smokehouse crow, only instead of wings there were paddles for the wind to turn. Josh held it high and ran with it down to the river; the paddles turned, and as they did they made a whistling sound. It was almost as if the whirligig had a life of its own. Josh was pleased with it, and with himself. He couldn't wait until he gave it to Mr. Wicker. He found a box for it and carefully wrapped it in fancy paper, and wrote on it, "Do not open until Xmas."

On the evening before vacation started, the dormitory was an anthill of activity. Some boys were busy packing while others were fooling around. One boy walked down the corridor with skis on, while another wore snowshoes with a bed sheet tied capelike around his neck.

There was talk of short-sheeting Barton Forbes' bed, but most of the boys agreed it was a dangerous idea. They said they would do it on the last day of school.

Josh was alone in his room when he heard someone yelling for help. At first he thought it was just someone fooling around, but when he recognized the voice, he ran out to investigate.

There in the middle of the corridor, dripping wet with only a towel around him, was Barton Forbes. He was pale and trembling. A group of boys gathered around him.

"I—I—saw it," he stuttered. "I saw the ghost of Fillmore Greenleaf."

If anyone else had said that, all the boys would have dismissed it as a joke. But everyone knew Barton Forbes had absolutely no sense of humor.

"He came at me from the wall!" Barton Forbes trembled when he spoke. "He looked scary. He was wearing an old uniform, and he had a long black beard. It was the most terrible thing I've ever seen."

The boys decided to form an investigating committee, but the more they talked about it the more they thought it would be best to proceed with their investigation in the morning.

That night all the lights burned in the dormitory and groups of boys gathered to discuss the situation. There were those who thought Barton Forbes had finally cracked, while others were convinced that there was a ghost.

Josh didn't know what to believe.

9

Word of the night's happening reached the commandant. In the morning before breakfast he assembled the boys and told them that he would order a thorough investigation of the situation. He also hinted that platoon leader Forbes was perhaps under great stress and strain.

Josh got things ready for his stay at Mr. Wicker's. Securing his belongings in the bicycle basket, he took off, happy to be leaving Cragsmoor.

At the final turn in the village Josh could see Mr. Wicker at the bridge in front of his house. He waved vigorously to Josh. Josh waved back and raced his bicycle. He was eager to tell Mr. Wicker about the ghost.

A frost covered the bridge, and beneath it water

gurgled under an icy coat. Otis Wicker gave Josh a cheery welcome and quickly ushered him into the house.

"There's much to do today," he said, leading Josh up the narrow stairway to the bedroom. He pointed to a pine chest of drawers in the room and told Josh that it was to be his for the stay. While Josh unpacked his belongings, Mr. Wicker excused himself and went into the kitchen.

Josh hurriedly placed his things in the old chest, and rushed down to join Mr. Wicker in the kitchen.

There was a small fire going in the fireplace, and Daphne sat on the hearth watching it. When Josh entered the room she turned her head from the fire and greeted him with a long low cry.

"Hi, Daphne," said Josh.

The good smell of cinnamon filled the room. Mr. Wicker removed a tray of warm biscuits from the oven.

"Some nourishment before our tree-hunting expedition," he said, filling a basket with the cinnamon and raisin biscuits.

Otis Wicker made everything seem a special occasion, and Josh enjoyed it. He listened as Mr. Wicker wondered aloud what type of Christmas tree they would search for.

"Blue spruce or fir?" he asked.

Josh didn't know much about the different kinds of evergreens, so he shrugged. "They both sound okay," he said.

But Mr. Wicker continued, "Perhaps hemlock or pine?"

Josh interrupted him. "There was a ghost at school last night, practically scared Forbes to death."

"Yes, I know," said Mr. Wicker matter-of-factly. Then he began to discuss Christmas decorations.

"You know?" asked Josh, surprised.

"Of course; news like that travels fast," said Mr. Wicker.

"Commandant Almstead thinks Forbes is seeing things," said Josh.

"Perhaps," said Otis Wicker. "But then again the commandant doesn't know everything." He poured tea into two large cups. "This ginger tea is marvelous with those biscuits. Be sure to put plenty of butter on them."

It seemed to Josh that if anyone knew what was really behind the Forbes ghost, it was old Mr. Wicker. Unwilling to let the subject drop, Josh asked, "What do you really think happened to Forbes in the shower room?"

"Not having been there, I really don't know," said Mr. Wicker. Josh was disappointed by his answer.

Otis Wicker got an axe, and they went outside for the tree hunt. Josh followed Mr. Wicker up the path that wound around the hill in back of the house. From the top he was able to see the Catskill Mountains and the meadows and fields that touched them. A cloud came in front of the sun, the sky darkened, and the sunshiny day was gone. An icy cold clung to the top of the hill. Josh suddenly felt as if he'd walked into another day.

They passed many evergreen trees which looked perfectly acceptable to Josh, but Mr. Wicker rejected them for reasons such as size, shape, or color.

At a clearing Josh was surprised to discover a little cemetery. A rusting iron fence circled several gravestones. "What a funny place for a cemetery," said Josh. "Why is it here?"

"Long ago, people used to be buried on their own land," Mr. Wicker said. He put down his axe and opened the iron gate.

Rust fell to the ground like paprika dust. "I guess no one has been here in a long time," Josh said, almost in a whisper.

"Yes, I suppose those who once remembered are gone too."

A sadness came to Josh. "It's almost like they never were," he said.

"They had their time, as we have ours now," said Mr. Wicker thoughtfully.

The grave markers were worn, and Josh stopped in front of one with a little lamb carved on it. He read the inscription on it, half aloud, half to himself. "Alden, beloved son of Clarence and Alice Lansberry, died in the fifth year of his life, June 1848. May his soul rest in heaven."

Josh had visions of a little boy rising from that spot toward the sky. He looked up, and a snowflake fell on his cheek.

"We'd better get our tree before we're buried in snow," said Mr. Wicker.

Outside the gate Josh noticed a flat stone. "That looks like a grave marker," said Josh. "It must have fallen. Why isn't it with the others?"

Mr. Wicker looked at the fallen grave marker and remained silent.

Snow dusted the cluster of brown moss and leaves that covered the grave. Josh kneeled and looked at the inscription. "So much of it is worn away," he said. "I can make out the letters. M–A. I think there is also an H and a W. There seems to be a date too, but it's hard to read."

Josh turned and looked at Mr. Wicker. He had a faraway expression on his face. The snow fell and caped the old man's shoulders, matching them to his hair and brows.

"It's sad to be buried all alone," said Josh. He wondered if he'd be buried near his mother or father. He had the terrible thought of neither one of them wanting him near them.

"Come on, Josh," said Mr. Wicker.

Josh walked alongside of Otis Wicker. He was silent.

"Cheer up, it's the season to be jolly." Mr. Wicker winked and smiled.

Josh smiled too.

Out of the clearing and in a wooded area again, they came upon a blue spruce. "Now that's what I call a nice tree," said Mr. Wicker and he took his axe to it.

Josh suddenly felt sorry for the tree, and he wanted to tell the old man to stop, but he didn't and the tree fell.

They carried the tree together, and on the

way back they stopped to gather some hemlock branches. "For a wreath," said Mr. Wicker.

When they passed the cemetery Josh placed a branch on the isolated grave. "Merry Christmas," he murmured.

By the time they reached the house it had become part of a snow-covered landscape. Small branches were beginning to bend under the weight of the heavy snowfall. Oliver greeted them on their arrival. He bounded through the snow, and ate it as if it were some special kind of dessert.

"We've got a tree," Josh said to the dog. "Can we show it to Oliver when it's all trimmed?" he asked, wanting desperately to take the dog inside the house.

"We'll see," said Mr. Wicker.

"I hope so," Josh said to himself.

10

"Mr. Wicker, someone's been in my room!" Josh shouted. He bounded down the narrow stairway.

"Nonsense," said Mr. Wicker calmly.

"But a drawer was open and it looked as if someone had been through it," said Josh, almost pleadingly.

"Blame it on Daphne," said Mr. Wicker. "She's terribly inquisitive."

"I left the drawer closed," said Josh.

Mr. Wicker held a tree stand in his hand. "Where shall we set the tree up?" he asked.

Josh looked at the old man and wondered if he had heard what he had said. "Mr. Wicker, the drawer was closed when I left the room."

"You might have thought the drawer was closed,

but if you had left it open just the slightest, Daphne would have worked at it until she got into it." Otis Wicker looked around the room. "Do you think we should put it near the fireplace?"

Josh remained quiet and looked at Mr. Wicker with a doubtful expression.

"Daphne loves socks," said the old man. "She'll do anything, and I mean anything, to get at them."

"It wasn't just the socks," Josh told himself. "Why did she rip the paper that covered the whirligig?" He couldn't tell Mr. Wicker about that without ruining his Christmas surprise for him.

He did say, "You mean Daphne can actually open a drawer?"

"Daphne might surprise you," said Otis Wicker.

"She already has," said Josh. He looked at the cat; she appeared very small curled up asleep in the wing chair.

"Well, Josh, you haven't told me where you think the tree should be."

Josh thought it strange of Mr. Wicker to ask his advice as to where the tree should go, since Otis Wicker was the kind of person who knew exactly where he wanted things.

It seemed that the old man wanted to get away

from the subject of the opened drawer. "Why don't you put the tree in the kitchen?" Josh said.

"Wonderful idea," exclaimed the old man.

The tree was set near the fireplace in the kitchen. Mr. Wicker brought out boxes of old Christmas decorations. He told Josh that some of them had belonged to his mother.

The idea of Mr. Wicker as a child with a mother seemed funny to Josh. He imagined the white-haired old teacher being wheeled around in a baby carriage, and he laughed to himself.

"Hard to believe I was once a child?" Mr. Wicker said, giving Josh a hawklike glance.

Josh swallowed hard. "Oh, no!" he said. And then he asked himself how the old man knew about what he was thinking. Was he guessing, or did he really know? Josh decided that if the old teacher was a mind reader, he had better be careful about what thoughts went on in his head when he was around him.

Josh began to think about his mother and father; he blamed them for his present situation. His thoughts turned to wishing he were somewhere else; then he remembered that there was the possibility of his mind being read, so he said in a very

74

cheerful voice, "Boy, am I having a good time."

"Good," said Mr. Wicker. "Now let's unpack these decorations."

The painted ornaments were carved of wood. They were of children, animals, and toys. "They're beautiful!" exclaimed Josh as he unwrapped a dappled pony.

"Thank you," said Otis Wicker. "I am very fond of them—they mean a great deal to me."

After all the ornaments were unwrapped Daphne came to inspect them. With a quick swipe of her paw a little Dutch boy went sailing across the room.

"Poor kid," said Josh, picking up the wooden ornament.

"Daphne, haven't you gotten into enough trouble for one day?" said Otis Wicker, picking up the cat and stroking her.

Trimming the tree was fun for Josh because Mr. Wicker let him do it his way. While Josh placed the ornaments on the tree, Mr. Wicker made garlands of cranberries and popcorn. When he finished that he brought out small candle holders —"For real candles on the tree," he said. Josh placed them about, fixing little candles into each one. Mr. Wicker helped weave the long garlands around the tree, and when that was done he gave Josh a jewel-like star for the very top of it.

After the tree was all trimmed Josh and Mr. Wicker sat back and looked at it. Josh looked at Mr. Wicker from the corners of his eyes, curious to see the old man's reaction. Otis Wicker had a warm smile on his face.

Pleased with himself and unable to remain silent, Josh said, "I think the tree looks very nice."

"Very nice?" shouted Mr. Wicker. "I think it looks splendid. And you shall be rewarded for your fine work with some fine fruitcake. I know I'm being boastful, but I do make delicious fruitcake."

Josh thought that there wasn't anything wrong with being honest about things one did well. He hated it when someone did something well and said it was awful in hopes of getting a compliment.

Mr. Wicker removed the fruitcake from a cupboard. It seemed to Josh as if the old man had placed his hands into some piece of magical equipment when the marvelous-looking cake appeared from the dark cupboard.

"Do you like roast duck?" Otis Wicker asked Josh.

"Sure," said Josh.

"Good, that's what we'll have for Christmas dinner. Cherry-glazed roast duck with wild rice."

Josh closed his eyes and almost imagined it. "That sounds great," said Josh. He bit into a large piece of fruitcake, and he began to think that Mr. Wicker was probably one of the most terrific cooks in the whole world.

Snow covered the windows and all outside views disappeared. "If it continues snowing like this, we'll be snowbound at Christmas," said Mr. Wicker. He sounded delighted at the thought.

Josh liked the idea of snow at Christmastime, but he wasn't too sure about being snowbound. It sounded a little scary not being able to go where you wanted. When Josh thought about it for a while he realized that he hadn't any other choice. There was no other place for him to go.

11

The kitchen glowed in the light from the Christmas tree. And the copper pots and pans that hung about the room mirrored the tree many times over. Josh caught his own reflection in an overhanging pan, and the distorted image he saw made him think of himself as a troll with an oversized nose. He stuck out his tongue, which made him take on an even more grotesque appearance.

While looking in the pan, he could see the fireplace behind him. A narrow cupboard door alongside it swung open; a cold chill made Josh cry out, and all the candles on the tree flickered.

"It's Santa stirring up a wind," said Mr. Wicker as he entered the room. "After all, it is Christmas Eve!" He slammed the cupboard door shut. And from another cupboard he removed three packages and placed them under the tree, next to the whirligig Josh had rewrapped and put there earlier.

Being snowbound with Mr. Wicker wasn't the awful experience that Josh thought it might be. He learned to make pineapple upside-down cake and chocolate chip cookies, which he liked a lot.

He also read. He read *The Legend of Sleepy Hollow* and *Rip Van Winkle*. When Mr. Wicker told him that those stories had been set in the surrounding countryside and that the author, Washington Irving, had lived along the Hudson River, Josh felt he had experienced something special.

Otis Wicker settled in a chair near the fireplace. Josh stood by and looked at the packages under the tree, wondering what was in them.

"There might not be any more Christmases here," sighed the old man.

Josh heard him, but his mind was still on the packages. Then he turned his attention to the cupboard alongside the fireplace and thought about the strong wind that had forced it open.

Mr. Wicker caught Josh's eye. "That's my preserve cupboard," he said. "Because part of it is built into the hill the temperature is always just perfect for my preserves."

Daphne jumped up on Mr. Wicker's lap and let out with some oriental meows.

The thought of Oliver all alone on such a night bothered Josh. He asked Mr. Wicker if he could invite the dog in.

Closing his eyes and almost appearing to go into a trance, Mr. Wicker remained silent. The silence lasted long enough for Josh to have regrets about asking for such a thing. He began to worry. "Mr. Wicker, are you all right?" he whispered.

Blinking his eyes and shaking his head as if awaking from a deep sleep, he said, "Of course we'll ask Oliver in. Christmas is the time for sharing."

Josh ran to the front door and threw it open. The light from the house poured out onto the sparkling snow. "Oliver!" Josh called. "Oliver, come here!" Josh's voice echoed. He wondered if Oliver was visiting with some other townspeople for the night. "Oliver!" he called once again, and waited. He strained his eyes hoping to see beyond the door light and into the darkness. "Oliver, it will soon be Christmas," he said.

The dog appeared at the bridge, his tail wagging and his amber eyes shining. "It's Christmas Eve,

Oliver. Come in. Daphne promised to behave herself." Oliver followed Josh into the house, and
Josh had a happy feeling.

Daphne eyed Oliver from Mr. Wicker's lap and
her silent greeting was proof enough that she would
get along with the dog, at least for that night.

Mr. Wicker got up from the chair and Daphne
remained in his place. "It's treat time," he said,
getting lost in the shadows of the kitchen. When he
reappeared he was holding a large tray piled high
with little cakes and cookies.

Oliver ate the most, with Josh a close second.
When the mantel clock chimed midnight, Mr.
Wicker said, "Now we can open our gifts."

Mr. Wicker excitedly opened his gift from Josh.
"A whirligig!" he shouted happily. His response
to the gift made Josh feel good.

Each of Mr. Wicker's gifts had a name written
across the top. There was one each for Josh,
Daphne, and Oliver. The one for Oliver surprised
Josh. He opened it for the dog—it was a leather
collar with his name on it. Josh put it around
Oliver's neck and wished he had thought of some-
thing like that. "It's from Mr. Wicker," said Josh.
"Thank him."

"It's from all of us, Oliver," the old man said,

nodding his head. The dog walked over to Mr. Wicker and placed his head under the leather-gloved hand. "Merry Christmas, Oliver," Mr. Wicker said and gently touched the dog with his other hand.

Daphne's gift was a calico mouse, which she immediately began to play with.

Josh's gift from Mr. Wicker was a watercolor set. He liked it a lot and told Mr. Wicker so. "I'll paint a picture of this house tomorrow," he said.

"And I'll put up the whirligig," said Mr. Wicker.

"It whistles in the wind," said Josh.

The candles on the tree burned low and Otis Wicker announced, "Bedtime!" He looked at Josh playing with Oliver. "Yes, you can take him up with you." He smiled.

Although it was dark and shadowy in the kitchen, Josh thought he saw Mr. Wicker place another package under the tree.

Oliver followed Josh upstairs. Inside the bedroom Josh jumped up and down on the bed and the dog joined him. A noise from downstairs made Josh stop and listen. The ruff around Oliver's neck stood on end and he growled, showing his teeth.

"It's only a door in the wind," said Josh, and he

buried himself under the covers. Oliver snuggled next to him.

The yellow room was sunshine bright in the early morning. Josh hurried out of bed and dressed. He raced downstairs, Oliver at his heels. The smell of bacon drifted from the kitchen.

"Merry Christmas," said Josh, going into the kitchen.

Otis Wicker looked up from the large skillet he was holding. He smiled and said, "Merry Christmas, Josh; Merry Christmas, Oliver." He gave the dog a big slice of bacon.

After breakfast they went outside, Mr. Wicker with the whirligig and Josh with his watercolors and a pad.

Icicles edged the smokehouse roof. Some of them cracked and fell as Josh and Mr. Wicker eased a ladder up against the cupola.

"A perfect place for the whirligig," said Mr. Wicker. He climbed up the ladder and fastened the whirligig to the very top of the cupola. A gentle wind quickly set the propeller in motion and the wings moved up and down.

Josh could hear the whistling sound. From on

top of the ladder Mr. Wicker shouted, "You're right; it whistles."

The crow appeared, and flew to the cupola roof to inspect his wooden look-alike. "Do you approve?" asked Otis Wicker, reaching into his pocket and coming up with a handful of birdseed.

The bird ate the seed and returned to his home under the eaves. "I'm sure he approves," said Mr. Wicker, "or else he would have scolded me angrily."

Just as Mr. Wicker stepped off the ladder, a red truck pulled up in front of the house. "Season's greetings!" the driver shouted from behind the wheel.

"Greetings to you," said Mr. Wicker, with a distant tone to his voice.

The driver was a big man; his complexion matched the truck. Two rifles rested in a rack in the cab.

Oliver, who was usually friendly, remained at Josh's side, and his tail went between his legs. "What's the matter?" Josh whispered.

The red-faced driver forced a big smile and, trying to take on a good-neighborly attitude, he said, "I noticed a whole family of squirrels in that maple tree you have up the road—pesky little things—and I wanted to ask you if I could do a little hunting there."

A quiet anger took hold of the old man. He narrowed his eyes and his lips barely moved as he said, "I've told you before. No hunting here!"

"Just thought I'd ask," said the driver. They watched as the truck disappeared around the bend.

Perspiration trickled down Otis Wicker's face. "That's Bob Dunham. Kills anything that moves."

Mr. Wicker went inside the house and Josh remained outside with his watercolors. While he painted a picture of the house, he suddenly felt the house was looking back at him. As he painted in the bedroom window he was aware of a dark shape moving behind the frosted glass.

He ran into the house. Mr. Wicker was seated at his desk. "Mr. Wicker," he cried, "I thought I saw something moving in the bedroom window."

"Daphne, no doubt," said the old man.

The cat appeared in the kitchen doorway. "It couldn't have been Daphne," Josh murmured.

12

Christmas dinner was served in the dining room with the fancy dishes and silver candlesticks. Josh was quiet.

"No need to be troubled, Josh," said Mr. Wicker while taking a second helping of rice. "Strange things seem to happen at snowy windows. It all has to do with light and shade and reflections. You know we discovered nothing when we investigated the room."

A chill enveloped Josh when he thought about how cold the room was when he had gone into it.

Mr. Wicker laughed. "Anyway, what did you expect to find, Greenleaf's ghost? I think he prefers Cragsmoor!"

Suddenly Josh felt silly and he laughed. The

troubled feeling left him, and he bit into a piece of roast duck.

When dinner was over Josh and Mr. Wicker played Scrabble in front of the living-room fireplace. They laughed when the first word Josh spelled was ghost.

There was a scratching at the door and Josh was happy to discover it was Oliver returning and wanting to spend the night. Mr. Wicker agreed to the dog's staying, and Josh was especially grateful, because he really didn't want to be all alone that night.

Josh went to sleep with his arm around Oliver, and he was awakened once by the dog's snoring. When the dark night sky began to fade Josh was up and out of bed. He went into the kitchen in hopes of surprising Mr. Wicker with breakfast, but he was already up and working at the stove.

"Sleep well?" the old man inquired.

Josh nodded Yes. "I thought I would surprise you and prepare breakfast," said Josh.

"Well, you can help," said Otis Wicker, and he handed Josh a bowl of eggs to scramble.

During breakfast Mr. Wicker told Josh he had

some important errands to take care of that day, and his housekeeper, Mrs. Mitchell, would probably stop by.

"She's an eccentric old creature," said Otis Wicker. "Just ignore her and she'll go about her business."

The idea of Mr. Wicker calling someone else an old creature seemed funny to Josh and he almost laughed aloud.

Otis Wicker left carrying an envelope. Josh waved good-bye to him from the front door, and Mr. Wicker turned on the bridge and said, "I won't be too long. Feel free to read any book in my library."

Josh watched as Mr. Wicker walked slowly through the snow, his green plaid coat the only color against the white of the village. Oliver cried to be let out, and Josh let him go. The dog bounded through the snow and was quickly out of sight.

The house was quiet except for the ticking of the clock and an occasional wind sound in the fireplace. Josh stood on a stool to investigate the upper shelves of the bookcase. Toby mugs and Chinese ginger jars sat between and on piles of books. Daphne viewed Josh from a high shelf; she was almost like a bookend wedged between stacks of books.

As Josh reached for a book he was startled by the front door opening. A small bent figure dressed in what appeared to be layers of rags entered the room. It was Mrs. Mitchell. She waddled to a chair and with great effort removed a pair of rubber boots. When she stood up she sighed, coughed, and stepped aside from her boots, which were quickly making a puddle on the rug.

Josh remained on the stool, looking on without saying a word. Mrs. Mitchell continued to remove her outer layers of clothing. She didn't look at Josh. Soon there were articles of her clothing on almost every piece of furniture in the room. When she got down to a gray baggy sweater and a purple-blue skirt she stopped undressing.

The strange-looking housekeeper went to Mr. Wicker's desk, looked through some papers, and muttered to herself.

"I guess the old man isn't here," she said, turning to Josh.

Josh hesitated before answering. He was surprised to hear her refer to Mr. Wicker as the old man.

"I'm Mrs. Mitchell," she said in a voice that had a whine to it.

"I'm Josh Newman."

"You're one of the boys from the school, ain'tcha?"

"Yes," answered Josh.

Mrs. Mitchell sat in the wing chair and took a cigarette out of her sweater pocket. It looked like it had been used before. She had some difficulty getting it lit, but once she did she inhaled deeply and let the smoke come out of her nose. While she smoked, the ashes fell to her skirt, which she brushed off onto the carpet. Josh was surprised by the housekeeper's behavior.

Tossing the cigarette butt in the fireplace, Mrs. Mitchell got up from the chair. She stretched, yawned, and said, "I guess I'd better get to work."

Josh thought she looked like a wrinkled child that was getting ready for bed.

Mrs. Mitchell went to a cupboard and removed a broom, a feather duster, and some rags that smelled of lemon oil. She kept muttering things to herself.

Then she spoke loud enough for Josh to hear her.

"The old man sure needs someone to look after him; he's a rotten housekeeper."

It was hard for Josh to believe this old woman was a better housekeeper than Mr. Wicker. He watched her work. She barely touched anything with the feather duster, and her sweeping was just moving some dust from one side of the room to the other. She passed the lemon-oil rags lightly over the furniture, and then collapsed exhaustedly in a kitchen chair.

"I'm dead!" she whined; then she looked at Josh and said, "Would you make me a cup of coffee?"

Josh knew she couldn't have been as tired as she pretended to be, and he wanted to say, "Make your own coffee." But he had never spoken back to an older person so he prepared the coffee and served it to her. The strange housekeeper took the coffee from Josh without even saying thank you. Josh wanted to tell her something about manners, but he didn't.

She drank her coffee from the saucer and complained that it was awful. While she was complaining an overhanging pan fell to the floor. It made a loud noise and the old woman jumped up, dropping the cup and saucer onto her lap.

"It's starting up again," she cried. "Last time the rug was pulled from under me."

The sugar bowl toppled and a spoon bounced off the table. It was difficult for Josh to hold back his laughter, but he controlled himself as best he could. At the same time he was puzzled. What had triggered off these accidents?

"I ain't cleaning up this mess," said Mrs. Mitchell. She ran into the living room, quickly gathering her layers of clothing, and in her rush she put her boots on the wrong feet. She slammed the door on her way out, getting a scarf caught in it. She pounded on the door for Josh to free her, and when he did, she shook her fist at him and said, "There's something funny going on in this house!"

Josh watched her through the window and it seemed as if her feet were going in a different direction from her body. Josh laughed out loud.

13

Josh remained at the window, and it gradually became a mirror for him. As he was looking at himself he became aware of a dark figure reflected behind him. The room grew cold.

Afraid to turn around, Josh continued to look at the window, hoping whatever it was would disappear. The unexpected sound of laughter shattered the silence and made Josh cry out. He turned around. There in the room with him was a black boy about his own age.

"Did I scare you?" said the boy.

Josh breathed deeply, and his throat was dry when he began to speak. "Sure you scared me," he said.

"I'm good at scaring people," the boy laughed.

"Well, I bet you'd be scared too if I came sneaking up on you!" said Josh.

"Maybe. But I'm better at it," said the boy boastfully.

The boasting annoyed Josh. "Who are you?" he asked. "And how did you get in?"

"I'm Matthew Hubbard," said the boy. "And I know who you are," he continued.

Josh narrowed his eyes and folded his arms across his chest. "Okay, who am I?" he said, hoping to trap the boy in a lie.

"You're Josh," Matthew said, pleased with himself.

"How do you know?" Josh asked, surprised.

"Oh, I know lots," said Matthew teasingly.

A strange smell hung over the room. It was a smell that Josh had never been aware of before. It reminded him of mushrooms. Josh eyed the boy suspiciously. He appeared almost dusty, and his clothing was threadbare.

"Where do you live?" asked Josh.

"Here," said Matthew.

"Here?" said Josh.

"And there," laughed Matthew.

A confused expression came upon Josh's face. He shrugged his shoulders and stammered, "B-b-but Mr. Wicker never told me about you."

"There's lots of things Mr. Wicker hasn't told you." Matthew smiled. It was a sly smile.

"How did you get in the house?" Josh asked, bewildered.

Matthew ignored Josh's question and called Daphne down from the shelf.

"Listen, Matthew Hubbard," said Josh, trying to sound tough, "how did you get in the house?"

"If you must know, from a cupboard," he said, and sat down on a stool with Daphne on his lap. "Daphne likes me."

Matthew's answer as to how he got into the house made Josh shake his head in disbelief. "I don't believe you entered this house through a cupboard," he said. Then he looked Matthew directly in the eye. "From what cupboard?"

Matthew Hubbard sighed impatiently. "Well, if you must know, I got in from the fireplace cupboard."

"The fireplace cupboard!" exclaimed Josh.

"Yeah, you see there's a tunnel behind it; it's connected to the smokehouse." Matthew got up and began to walk toward the kitchen. "Come, I'll show you," he said.

"But that's Mr. Wicker's preserve cupboard," said Josh.

"It is, but it's also something else," said Matthew.

At first Josh was reluctant to follow Matthew into the kitchen, but he was curious, so he did.

Matthew looked at the Christmas tree and said, "Nicest tree Mr. Wicker's had since he's lived in this house."

Josh figured Matthew Hubbard had to be lying, because he knew that Mr. Wicker had lived in the house a very long time. Longer than Matthew could remember.

Taking on a pose like a salesman demonstrating some household appliances, Matthew stood near the fireplace cupboard.

He opened the cupboard door. "Now what do you see?" he said to Josh, winking.

Josh looked at the labeled jars that crammed the shelves. "I see lots of preserves," he said.

Then Matthew showed Josh that the preserve shelves were built onto a door. He opened it easily with a small knob alongside one of the shelves.

When the door swung open Josh found himself looking into a cold, dark tunnel.

Matthew stood at the mouth of the tunnel. "Come

with me," he said. He motioned with his hand for Josh to join him.

Josh trembled; he was cold and frightened.

"Come on," said Matthew, taking another step back into the tunnel.

"No," murmured Josh.

"Afraid?" said Matthew.

Frightened and unwilling to let the boy know that he was, Josh said, "Maybe some other time, but it's really too cold now."

Josh couldn't understand why Matthew Hubbard wasn't cold. He was poorly dressed for winter.

Slowly Matthew Hubbard began to disappear into the darkness.

"Where are you going?" said Josh. "There is something I want to ask you," he whispered.

Matthew vanished, the cupboard door slammed shut, and Josh remained frozen in front of it. A musty smell hovered about the kitchen.

A noise at the front door moved Josh from his rigid position. He ran to the door. It was Oliver, and Josh was happy to see the dog. "Oliver, the strangest thing just happened," he said, hugging him. Oliver remained at the doorway and when

Josh tried to lead him into the room he backed away growling.

"Oliver, what's the matter?" said Josh.

Otis Wicker appeared at the open doorway. "What is going on?" he asked.

Josh let go of the dog, and he ran out and across the bridge.

"Is Mrs. Mitchell still here?" asked Mr. Wicker.

"No," answered Josh. He was eager to tell Mr. Wicker about Matthew Hubbard, but just as he was about to, he was interrupted.

"Was Mrs. Mitchell here?" Mr. Wicker asked.

"Yes, she was here," said Josh. "And she was frightened off."

"Frightened off?" said Mr. Wicker, removing his hat and coat. "Is that crazy lady imagining things again?"

Otis Wicker went into the kitchen and began taking down pots and pans. "We're going to have a marvelous lunch," he said.

"Mr. Wicker, you have a guest in your house," said Josh.

Otis Wicker put down the pots and pans. He looked at Josh wide-eyed. "You know?"

"Yes, I know," said Josh.

"And you're not afraid?" asked Mr. Wicker.

"Why should I be afraid?" said Josh.

"Well, almost everyone is afraid of a ghost."

"Ghost?" exclaimed Josh. "I said guest."

"But my guest is a ghost," said Mr. Wicker.

"Oh no!" whispered Josh. He felt his head grow tight, and his skin turned to goose bumps.

Mr. Wicker looked at Josh, his brows knitted together, and nodded his head Yes.

14

The afternoon sun made the house glow in shades of russet and copper. Mr. Wicker and Josh sat in the living room; Josh listened as the old teacher spoke to him and tried to explain things.

It took Otis Wicker a long time to persuade Josh he had nothing to be afraid of, and since there wasn't any place he could go, he should just try to make the best of it.

"Matthew Hubbard is harmless," said Mr. Wicker. "He may be a trickster at times, but he'd never do anything terrible. He doesn't like Mrs. Mitchell; that's why he pulls the pranks he does on her."

"I don't like her either," said Josh. "I didn't know what was happening at the time, but now that I've found out what it was all about, I'm glad Matthew pulled what he did with Mrs. Mitchell. She's a terrible old lady."

Josh thought that Matthew Hubbard was likable; he just didn't like the idea of him being a ghost. He told that to Mr. Wicker.

"If you hadn't found out about Matthew being what he is, I'm sure you'd be friendly toward him. Just treat him like you would some boy at the Academy," said Mr. Wicker.

Josh sighed deeply. "It will be hard to think of him as some boy at Cragsmoor, but I'll try."

"When you get to know Matthew I'm sure you'll get along fine. He has ESP," Mr. Wicker said, almost like a proud grandfather.

"ESP?" Josh repeated.

Otis Wicker laughed. "ESP means extrasensory perception. He is just capable of knowing about some things in advance, or what you might be thinking. He apparently receives strong vibrations from you."

The idea of a ghost knowing about him bothered Josh. "You can tell Matthew that I'm not going to give him any more vibrations," said Josh.

"I really don't think we have much control over

things like that," Mr. Wicker said. "It was Matthew who told me that you were on your way here one afternoon. He whispers in my ear sometimes to let me know what someone is thinking. He's been around; it's just that you haven't been aware of him before. I also have a confession to make." Mr. Wicker looked like a boy who had been caught passing a note in class. "It was Matthew who told me of your plans to run away. I hid your bicycle, Josh." Mr. Wicker threw his hands back. "I'm glad it's all out in the open now."

"Me too!" said Matthew, appearing in the doorway.

"Hello, Matthew," said Mr. Wicker.

"Thanks for the Christmas present," said Matthew.

"I hope you like the brand," said Mr. Wicker. "Matthew, I think you owe Josh a thank-you too."

Josh was startled once again by Matthew's sudden appearance, and confused by his conversation with Mr. Wicker.

"Oh, thanks for putting the hemlock on my grave," said Matthew.

"Was that your grave?" asked Josh.

Matthew nodded his head Yes and removed a small tin from his pocket. "It's chewing tobacco," said Matthew. "That's what Mr. Wicker gave me for Christmas."

"I thought I saw you put something under the tree Christmas Eve," exclaimed Josh.

"Yes, it was my gift for Matthew," said Mr. Wicker.

Josh couldn't quite believe what was happening, and it almost made him dizzy. "I can't believe it," he said aloud.

"That's what I said when I first moved into this house and met Matthew, but I quickly adjusted," said Mr. Wicker.

"Do you know old Greenleaf?" Josh asked Matthew.

Matthew shook his head. "Never heard of him; who is he?"

"He's supposed to be a gho—" Josh interrupted himself. "I mean he's in the same condition you are."

"Heck, you can say it; he's a ghost same as me. Never heard of him." Matthew put some tobacco in his mouth and began to chew.

"What does it taste like?" asked Josh, who thought it looked awful.

"Want some?" said Matthew, handing the tin to Josh.

"No thanks," cried Josh. "It might ruin my appetite."

"Never stopped me from eating," said Matthew.

"Which reminds me!" cried Mr. Wicker, getting up from his chair. "We never did have our lunch, and here it is dinnertime already. Poor Josh, you must be starving." Otis Wicker went into the kitchen, leaving Josh and Matthew alone.

The image of a slow death by starvation and then becoming a ghost filled Josh's thoughts. He tried to clear his mind, because the idea of dying and becoming a ghost frightened him.

Matthew stood by the fireplace and spat some tobacco into it. His back was toward Josh as he said, "You'll have to die sometime. Anyway, not everyone who dies becomes a ghost."

Josh knew that Matthew was picking up his thoughts at that moment and there wasn't anything he could do about it. "I don't think I'll mind dying when I'm old," said Josh. "I'm just not ready for it now. I mean there's so many things to do." It suddenly occurred to Josh that Matthew had probably died without doing all the things he wanted to do, and he felt sorry for him.

"How come you're a ghost?" Josh asked.

"I don't know," said Matthew. "But I sure wish

I wasn't one, so that I could go to wherever I have to."

"How did you die?" asked Josh.

"I think I fell from a tree, or was it from the roof of the smokehouse?—I don't remember right now," said Matthew.

"Do you remember when you died?" said Josh.

"Nope, I don't even know when I was born," said Matthew.

"You mean you never had a birthday party?" cried Josh.

"Now what kind of question is that? Of course not! How can you have a birthday party when you don't know when you were born?" Matthew looked at Josh and shook his head. "Boy, you are some dummy."

"You're calling me a dummy when you don't even know your own birthday," shouted Josh.

"Anyway, what's so important about a dumb old birthday?" said Matthew. He jumped up on a table, knocking over a candlestick.

"What's going on out there?" Mr. Wicker shouted from the kitchen.

"Josh here just knocked over a candlestick," said Matthew.

"I did not," said Josh.

"He's lyin', Mr. Wicker," shouted Matthew. He held his hand over his mouth and laughed.

Otis Wicker walked into the living room with a big wooden mixing spoon in his hand and shook it at Josh and Matthew. "Let's stop the nonsense; dinner is ready."

"I'm not hungry," said Matthew. He remained behind as Josh and Mr. Wicker went into the kitchen.

Mr. Wicker whispered to Josh, "Whenever I ask Matthew to eat he always says he's not hungry. There's really no need for him to eat, but I always ask him just the same so he doesn't feel left out."

"I didn't knock over the candlestick," whispered Josh.

"I know," said Mr. Wicker. "Matthew is really kind of touchy on the subject of birthdays. But he was born a slave, and if there was any record of his birth date it's gone."

"He was born a slave?" Josh whispered.

Mr. Wicker nodded Yes and handed Josh a plate piled high with food.

15

Josh spent a restless night wondering what would make Matthew go to where he had to, so that he wouldn't be a ghost anymore. He lay in bed until he could see the bird-and-thistle design on the walls. Downstairs he heard Mr. Wicker and Matthew talking.

"I know it's a serious problem," said Mr. Wicker. "But I am trying every possible way imaginable to save this house. Yesterday I mailed out documents to the state authorities, hoping to establish the historical significance of this property."

"I'm afraid!" cried Matthew. "What will happen to me?" Josh listened from outside the room as Matthew sobbed quietly. Josh hated to hear anyone cry. He wanted to get out of the house so that

Matthew would not be embarrassed by his being there. Josh knew that when he had to cry he didn't want anyone around.

Quietly Josh dressed and made it to the front door, but just as he turned the latch, Mr. Wicker called out, "Where are you going, Josh?"

Josh bit down on his lip. "Darn," he murmured, upset with himself for not making a better getaway.

Mr. Wicker walked into the room. "Where were you going?" he asked again.

"I—I was going to look for Oliver," said Josh. "I was wondering where he was." Although Josh was using Oliver as an excuse, it suddenly occurred to him that he hadn't seen the dog in a while.

Otis Wicker slumped in the desk chair. "No need to worry about Oliver; I'm sure he's fine," he said.

Matthew came into the room and said, "Mornin', Josh." It was easy to tell that he was in a gloomy mood. He sat down in the wing chair and fixed his eyes on the floor.

"Morning, Matthew," said Josh, feeling uncomfortable because he knew something was really wrong.

Otis Wicker looked at Josh, and Josh could see that the old teacher was worried and tired. He spoke wearily. "I've been trying to avoid thinking about or discussing the fate of this house. I really didn't want to face it myself, and I didn't want to bother you with it, Josh; but I'm afraid I've got a great problem."

"Is there anything I can do to help?" said Josh.

"I don't know. And it's not myself I'm concerned about—I can go anywhere. It's Matthew that troubles me." Mr. Wicker looked in Matthew's direction; his mouth turned downward and his eyes got watery.

Josh almost felt like crying himself.

"All we can do now is wait to hear from the state highway commission. Perhaps after looking through my findings they might find this house worthy of being saved." Mr. Wicker forced a smile. "Sausage and eggs, anyone?"

"I'm not hungry," said Matthew.

"Let me prepare breakfast," said Josh.

Too tired to protest, Mr. Wicker agreed.

During breakfast Josh learned that the house had once been a part of the Underground Railway for escaped slaves.

"The tunnel connecting the kitchen with the smokehouse was a perfect place for hiding people," said Mr. Wicker.

"Is that how Matthew got here?" asked Josh.

Matthew came into the kitchen and sat on the stove. "My Aunt Hannah brought me here. She helped lots of slaves escape up north." He said it proudly.

"His aunt was Hannah Hubbard, one of the leaders in the Underground Railway. And this canal house was her base of operations."

Josh looked around the room and imagined the secret things that had happened in it. "They can't tear it down!" he shouted.

Daphne jumped on the table and carried a sausage away. "I don't blame her," said Mr. Wicker. "You are an excellent cook, Josh."

When everything was cleared away, Mr. Wicker read the morning paper and Josh let Matthew use his watercolors. Josh watched as Matthew sat at the bedroom window and painted a picture of the whirligig.

When Josh asked Matthew why he chose to paint the whirligig, Matthew told Josh that he had once started to make one himself, only he had never finished his—he couldn't remember why.

Josh thought Matthew's painting was terrific, and he was happy when Matthew said that he could keep it. Mr. Wicker came into the bedroom with the newspaper in his hand.

"There's a special New Year's show at the Mayfair Theater in Pinewood Plains," said Mr. Wicker, and he showed Josh the advertisement in the paper.

Josh read it aloud. " 'Gala New Year's show, live entertainment! Musicians, magicians, and clowns.' Sounds like fun."

"We'll go," said Mr. Wicker.

"Sounds terrible," said Matthew.

"Don't you want to go?" said Josh excitedly, and then he put his hand to his mouth. "I'm sorry, I forgot."

"Even if I could go, I wouldn't," said Matthew. He left the bedroom and went into the kitchen, disappearing behind the fireplace cupboard.

"Wait, Matthew!" shouted Josh. He ran down to the kitchen and opened the cupboard door.

"NO!" shouted Mr. Wicker from the kitchen doorway. He put his hand to his heart and took a deep breath. "You run fast, Josh." He sighed. Otis Wicker was pale and he sat down in a chair. Josh saw that he was trembling.

"What's wrong?" he asked.

"You must never go beyond that cupboard door —that's Matthew's world. It's not for us." He sighed deeply again. "Just in time," he whispered.

16

Two days passed without any sign of Oliver. When Josh said he was worried about the dog, Mr. Wicker and Matthew told Josh not to worry. It was difficult for Josh not to think about him.

Josh wondered if Matthew's being around had anything to do with Oliver's disappearance. During this time Matthew went out of his way to be extra nice to Josh. He painted pictures for him of scenes he remembered from the past. He painted one of himself on top of a horse.

"It's Blossom. She and her sister Bedilia were a team of canal horses; they pulled the barge *Sweet April*." Then Matthew painted a picture of the barge. He put three people on the deck. "That's Captain Ferguson, and his wife and their daughter Molly. Molly dared me to stand on top of Blossom, and I did, and I fell into the canal." Matthew scratched the top of his head. "And I think I drowned," he said.

"You died by drowning?" asked Josh. "I thought you fell from a tree—or was it the smokehouse roof?"

"Is that what I said?" Matthew looked puzzled.

"Yes, that's what you said," answered Josh.

"Well, maybe I ain't a ghost at all, just pretendin' to be one." Matthew laughed.

"Then you sure are putting on a darn good show," said Josh. A moment of doubt came to him.

Matthew handed Josh the watercolors. "Now you paint something for me," he said.

Josh painted a picture of Cragsmoor for Matthew. "Now *that* place looks scary," said Matthew.

"It is," said Josh.

A letter arrived for Mr. Wicker informing him that he was to appear in Albany on January 10th to present his case for the preservation of the house. Josh wished that he could think of a way to help Matthew so that he wouldn't be a ghost any longer.

After reading the letter, Mr. Wicker said, "You'll see—things will be fine."

The gloomy mood that hung over the house

changed. And Josh said, "It will be a fine New Year's."

"Yes," said Mr. Wicker. "And to start it off, Josh, you and I are going to the show at the Mayfair Theater. When we return we'll all have a New Year's party."

Matthew agreed to the idea and told them to have a good time.

Josh went with Mr. Wicker to get his car, which was in a garage a short distance from the house. Mr. Wicker's car looked almost as old as he did. It needed a paint job, there was a big dent in a front fender, and the door on the driver's side didn't open. When Josh saw the car he was sure it would never leave the garage, and he was surprised when it started up without any trouble.

"Runs as good as the day I got her," said Mr. Wicker. Josh thought Mr. Wicker looked funny driving—his eyes were barely above the steering wheel. He drove very slowly so most people passed him, and when they did they looked into the car to see who was driving. "We're not in any rush," said Mr. Wicker. "We'll get to the theater with plenty of time to spare."

By the time they got to town the streetlights

had been turned on. It was easy to find the May-fair Theater, since it was the only theater in Pine-wood Plains. Words were crowded on the small marquee, making it look like all the letters of the alphabet were scrambled on it. There were just a few people standing around the box office; Josh figured that there weren't too many people eager to see the Gala New Year's show.

The theater seats creaked, and Josh told himself that the Mayfair had probably been decorated about the same time Mr. Wicker got his automobile, and they were both in the same sad-looking condition.

The lights dimmed in the theater, and the stage lights were turned on. They showed a shell-pink satin curtain with a huge dark stain that reminded Josh of the map of South America.

A three-piece band on one side of the stage played noisily. The music stopped when a tall skinny man in an ill-fitting tuxedo walked out onto the stage. He introduced himself as the manager of the Mayfair Theater and then announced the first act, which was a lady ventriloquist with a dummy.

The ventriloquist was awful, and Josh found himself thinking about the boys at the Academy whom he'd be seeing in another day. He wondered what they would think of his ghost story—but Josh didn't want to tell it to anyone. It was a secret that he wanted to keep.

By the time the ventriloquist was through with her act the few people there were in the audience had begun to speak to each other.

When she left the stage, the manager returned and announced the next act as "the one you've all been waiting for. Ladies and gentlemen," he said, "Roland the Mysterious Macabre Wizard of Magic."

The pink satin curtain was drawn aside and the stage was all in black. A figure in a black cape with its back to the audience stood in the center of the stage. There was a long drum roll, and when it stopped the figure turned around.

Otis Wicker let out a cry and Josh gasped. They looked at each other in disbelief.

Roland was black, and his resemblance to Matthew was so great that if having an older twin brother was possible, Roland the magician would have been Matthew's brother.

Roland the magician brought out a girl, his assistant. She blindfolded him and went into the audience. When she held up different objects Roland was able to identify them. He also pulled doves, scarves, flowers, and umbrellas from a teapot. For his finale Roland sawed his assistant in half.

On the way home Josh said to Mr. Wicker, "Do you think Roland the magician's last name might be Hubbard, and Matthew is his ancestor?"

"Possibly," said Mr. Wicker. It began to snow, and Josh watched it fall in the headlight beam. Mr. Wicker drove more slowly than before; his mind didn't seem to be on his driving—his thoughts were somewhere else. He was silent for most of the trip. It wasn't until the car was in the garage that he turned and looked at Josh. "I wonder if there is such a thing as reincarnation?" he said.

"Maybe we were all somebody else at a different time," said Josh, "and we just don't know it." Josh began to wonder who he might have been. Josh was hoping that Oliver would be waiting for him at the house, and when he wasn't there he told Mr. Wicker that he was going to look for the dog in the morning.

The house was still when they entered it. Josh followed Mr. Wicker into the kitchen and they both cried out, startled by Matthew, who banged on a pot and shouted, "Happy New Year!"

They all had a good laugh, and together they shouted, "Happy New Year!"

"Quite a trickster!" said Mr. Wicker.

Josh and Mr. Wicker looked at each other, and at that moment Matthew took a deep bow and smiled.

17

The snow fell all night, and in the morning there was a new coat of white on everything. For the first time during his stay there Josh was up before anyone else. He dressed and went outside.

The pearl-gray color at dawn remained for the morning sky. It was New Year's Day, Josh's last with Mr. Wicker. Josh began to walk up the hill behind the house. He listened to the soft sound his footsteps made on the snow, and he turned often to look at his tracks. He wished he could erase them because he felt he was ruining something special by disturbing the even covering.

He was glad Mr. Wicker hadn't asked him anything about New Year's resolutions. Josh was good at keeping secrets, but it was difficult for him to keep promises to himself. Not doodling in his text-books was one of them.

At the top of the hill Josh looked down upon the house. It was nestled snugly in the snow. Josh thought about how its outward appearance gave no hint that it had a ghost living in it.

Because of Matthew, Josh had convinced himself that old Greenleaf was probably running around at the Academy. He wondered if he would see him also.

The little cemetery on top of the hill was almost hidden. Josh stood at the iron gate and said, "It's another year, folks."

He remained at the cemetery for a while, and it occurred to him that one day he too would be buried, and that life did have an end. He found himself making a New Year's resolution. "I'm going to make the most of every day," he told himself.

He walked away from the cemetery and began to think of ways to make time count. He decided that one of the things he was going to do was read a lot so that he would know about many things. He also thought that he would try to help people who couldn't help themselves.

A sudden wind came across the hilltop and shook the snow from the branches, making it seem as if it were snowing again. Josh made a path under a long row of maple trees, and when the wind rushed through them, he turned his face upward and closed his eyes. He laughed as the snow tickled his face.

At the edge of the maples Josh noticed a small mound of snow shaped like a sleeping animal. An awful feeling came over Josh. He kneeled and brushed at the snow. When he uncovered a patch of honey-colored hair, he cried out. With tears running down his face, Josh removed all the snow from the animal. It was Oliver—he had been shot.

Josh carried the dog down the hill, sobbing. Mr. Wicker and Matthew were at the door. They greeted Josh with watery eyes.

"Matthew knew about it two days ago when it happened," Mr. Wicker cried.

"I just didn't want to tell you, Josh. I couldn't," sobbed Matthew.

"It's the hunters," said Mr. Wicker. "If they don't get deer, or rabbits, or squirrels, they get frustrated and they'll shoot at anything."

"Poor Oliver," Josh cried, unwilling to put the dog down.

Mr. Wicker came out of the house and took Oliver from Josh's arms. "The ground is frozen; we can't bury him now," he said, and then he went into one of the sheds.

Josh ran into the house and upstairs. He closed the bedroom door and sat with his back against it, crying.

Matthew knocked on the bedroom door. At first Josh told him to go away, but when Matthew said, "I want to tell you something," Josh let him in.

"I knew a raccoon once," said Matthew, sitting down on the bed. "And I found him dead in a trap some hunters had set. I still think about him."

Matthew's lower lip quivered and he seemed to fight back a cry. "Oliver didn't become a ghost, but if he had I'd have taken care of him." Big tears rolled down his face. He continued to speak. "Maybe one day I won't be a ghost anymore and can go where I have to. If I see Oliver there, I promise I'll look after him."

Images of a great indoor market place came to Josh. He imagined it filled with people and animals. And he pictured Matthew with Oliver.

Josh didn't eat all that day, and when Mr. Wicker said, "You've got to have something," Josh said, "I don't want anything. I'm not hungry."

That night Matthew told stories of times he remembered on the canal. He also sang a silly song that the canalmen sang—he wanted to cheer Josh up. Matthew sang in a clear, sweet voice.

The cook we had upon the deck
Stood six feet in her socks.
Her hand was like an elephant's ear;
Her breath would open locks.
A maid of sixty summers she
As handsome as a pig
And every time she'd go to sleep
Oh, Moses, how she'd snore!

When Matthew finished singing, Josh forced a smile and told him he thought it was a good song. He didn't want Matthew to feel that his song hadn't cheered him up.

Before going to bed that night, Josh packed his belongings. He stayed awake most of the night thinking about Oliver, and he wondered if when he died he would see the dog again.

In the morning the Christmas tree was gone. Matthew toyed with the star; he seemed unhappy, and when it was time to say good-bye to Josh he said, "Please come back soon."

After Josh's bicycle was secured on a rack on top

of Mr. Wicker's car, they drove back to Cragsmoor together. Josh didn't speak during the drive back, and more than once Mr. Wicker seemed about to say something, but he didn't.

At Cragsmoor they walked from the parking area along the path that went down to the river. Mr. Wicker put his hand on Josh's shoulder, and they walked that way for a while.

Mr. Wicker broke the silence. "I know how badly you feel about Oliver, but in the time you knew each other you were both happy, and I'm sure he died with only good memories; and that's important."

"He really liked me a lot, didn't he?" said Josh.

"Yes, you're a very likable boy, Josh," said Mr. Wicker.

Josh looked up at Otis Wicker and smiled.

The sound of laughter and shouting cut through the quiet morning. Some returning boys were playing touch football on the snowy field.

18

Miles Carpenter hadn't returned yet, and Josh sat alone in the cold green room, feeling trapped. The things he had taken along from Mr. Wicker remained packed. He lay on his bed and looked around the room; it was almost as if he were in it for the first time. He told himself that when he had his own place he would fill it with terrific antiques, things like Mr. Wicker had.

As he lay on his bed he spied a picture slide under Miles' bed. At first he wasn't going to make the effort to get it, but the more he thought about it the more curious he became. He rolled off his bed onto the floor and held the slide up to the window light.

It was the picture of the Civil War officer that

Josh had seen in Miles' library book. Josh returned to his bed; every once in a while he looked at the slide and wondered about its purpose.

When Josh heard Miles coming he tossed the slide back under his bed. Miles came into the room. His arms were loaded with packages, suitcases, and a hockey stick. His ice skates were around his neck. He greeted Josh with "Happy New Year, old bean!"

Miles piled his stuff on top of his bed and sat down on Josh's. He began to tell Josh about his vacation, and the new girl who had moved into his neighborhood. When he asked Josh about his holiday, Josh said, "It was good." He thought of Matthew and Oliver for a long time. He couldn't put them out of his mind.

Word had gotten around that Barton Forbes wasn't coming back. Rumors went around saying that Forbes had had a nervous breakdown, and some said they had heard he would have to spend the rest of his life in a straitjacket.

When mail call was held by another upperclassman, all the rumors about Barton Forbes were believed. Josh was surprised to receive a letter from his father. But when he opened it, it was a birth announcement with a picture of a newborn baby. "Meet your brother" was written across the back of it.

"He's not my brother," Josh murmured as he looked at the photograph. He tore it up along with the announcement.

Before classes began again, Commandant Almstead gathered all the boys in the chapel to report on what he called "Operation Ghost."

He told the boys that after a thorough investigation, he was convinced that the ghost thing was a hoax. They had discovered that someone had been in the shower-room supply closet and had left behind an electrical extension cord, leading them to believe that the ghost image had been conjured up in some way. The commandant also said that when they found the culprit he would be severely punished. He said if the boys had any information about it they should voluntarily come to him with it.

Josh thought about Miles and his slide projector, and the picture of the Civil War officer, and he knew he was the one responsible for Greenleaf's ghost.

The slide was still under Miles' bed when Josh returned to their room. He picked it up and put it in his pocket. When Miles returned, Josh took out the slide and held it up. "Mr. Carpenter, you'd better be more careful," he said, giving it to Miles.

Miles' face paled. "You won't say anything, will you?" he cried.

"Are you kidding? Of course I must tell the commandant." Josh said it with a serious expression on his face.

"Come on, Josh, I'll give you anything not to tell," Miles pleaded.

"Anything?" said Josh.

"Anything," answered Miles.

Josh squinted his eyes and looked around the room. "Let's see now," he whispered. "What do I want?" Miles swallowed hard, and Josh thought he looked as if he was about to cry.

"I want your hockey stick," said Josh.

"My hockey stick?" shouted Miles. He sighed deeply. "Is that all? It's yours!"

"You can keep your dumb hockey stick," said Josh. "I'm not going to tell anyone anything."

Miles looked dazed. "You really mean that? You promise?"

"Yes, I mean it. I promise," said Josh. "I guess you don't know me too well."

"I guess I don't," said Miles. He looked at Josh

for a while without saying anything, and then he put out his hand to him.

Josh and Miles shook hands. "You really are a pal," said Miles.

Josh felt embarrassed by Miles' sudden burst of friendship. He said, "It's the least I can do for a roomy, and I know you'd never rat on me."

"Yes I would," teased Miles.

"You'd better not," said Josh and he threw Miles to the floor. They wrestled until it was lunchtime, and then they went to the dining room together.

The days following the vacation were spent studying for exams. And when Josh saw Mr. Wicker he'd ask about Matthew.

Mr. Wicker told Josh that Matthew always asked about him.

On the day after the last exam, Josh went to Mr. Wicker's house. He walked there, and as he approached the village a sadness touched him. He wanted to shout out loud, "Oliver, I'm here." Although he knew the dog was gone, a moment of hope came to Josh and he thought he would see Oliver again.

Matthew gave Josh a big greeting and he told him he missed him. He also told Josh that Mr.

Wicker had given him a watercolor set. Matthew showed Josh his newest paintings. One was of a little black girl with a kitten, and the other was of a man playing a banjo. "They are people I remember," he said.

"They're really good," said Josh excitedly. "Maybe when you grow up you'll be famous."

"I ain't growing up, Josh," said Matthew.

Josh felt funny. "I forgot," he said apologetically. "I guess I just got carried away—but you are a good artist, Matthew."

Mr. Wicker served hot soup. While eating, Josh told them about his new half brother. "They sent me a picture of him," he said. "He's really ugly."

"All little babies are ugly," said Matthew.

Afterward they all sat in front of the fireplace. Mr. Wicker kept getting up to stoke the fire, and gradually Matthew grew sullen. Josh sensed an uneasiness. When Mr. Wicker said, "We'll know about the fate of this house in a few days," Josh knew for sure what was troubling them.

He said, "You'll never have to worry about this place."

"I hope you're right, Josh," said Matthew.

19

Barton Forbes returned to Cragsmoor with his leg in a cast; he had broken it skiing. At mail call when he sniffed the pink envelope for Josh his crutch fell to the floor. No one made any attempt to pick it up for him. And when mail call was over the boys stood around and watched as Forbes struggled to get at it.

Josh's mother wrote and told him about the glorious time she had had during the holidays, and how tanned she was. She also told Josh about all the fabulous people she met. A PS at the end of the letter told Josh not to make any plans for Easter. "We'll have a sensational time then," his mother said.

Josh made a plane out of the letter and aimed it

at the dart board. It glided and fell short of its target.

On the day Mr. Wicker was to go to Albany to present his case, Josh went to the house after classes.

Mr. Wicker hadn't returned yet. Josh sat in the wing chair and Daphne jumped in his lap. Matthew paced about the room restlessly.

Josh stroked the cat and told Matthew to calm down.

"I'm scared, Josh. I've been here over a hundred years; where do I go?"

Although Josh knew that Matthew was really a ghost it was hard for him to believe he had been around for more than a hundred years. The thought overwhelmed him. He sighed deeply and said, "Wow, that's a very long time." He looked at Matthew hard and long. "You really were a slave!" He said it almost to convince himself.

"Sure," said Matthew. "I didn't know it until one day I heard my mama praying, asking for us to be free. And when I asked her about it, she told me what we were. Then my Aunt Hannah came along and my mother sent me with her, and when she said good-bye she told me I would grow up to be a free man."

The thought of people owning people seemed impossible to Josh, but he knew it had once happened.

Matthew stuffed some tobacco into his mouth and chewed it for a bit and continued talking. "I never saw my mama again after I left with Aunt Hannah."

"I never see my mother," whispered Josh.

Matthew frightened Josh when he jumped up unexpectedly, as if he had heard something. He ran out of the room and into the kitchen, disappearing into the tunnel. Josh got up and ran after him. "Matthew, what is it?" Josh called into the cold darkness.

Mr. Wicker was standing at the kitchen door when Josh turned around. "Come away from there, Josh," he said. From the expression on the old man's face, Josh knew how things had gone at the hearing. Otis Wicker looked very worn and worried. He hadn't bothered to remove his overcoat, and he almost seemed to sink into it.

"I tried," he said wearily. "But they told me roads to airports are more important."

"I hate airports," cried Josh.

Josh knew that Matthew's ESP had told him what the decision had been. "What about Matthew?" he asked.

Mr. Wicker shook his head sadly. "I don't know."

Josh looked at the old teacher. "What about you?" he asked.

Otis Wicker smiled weakly. "I'm ready for retirement," he said. "I can go anywhere."

"When must you leave?" asked Josh.

"Early spring," said the old man. "It's pretty here then—there are daffodils that grow clear up to the top of the hill."

When Josh left, Mr. Wicker was still sitting in the chair wearing his coat. Josh felt helpless. He wished he could help Mr. Wicker and Matthew. If Matthew could stop being a ghost, Mr. Wicker wouldn't be so upset.

Outside, Josh walked slowly up the road, turning often to look at the house. It appeared suspended against the snowy hill. Josh couldn't understand how anyone could destroy a house such as that one.

A few days later it was Josh's birthday. In the morning he found a card on his pillow. It said, "Happy Birthday to a true friend." It was signed by Miles. Josh put the card in a large envelope, the one that also held Matthew's painting.

In art class that day Josh had an idea. He made a birthday card. When classes were finished Josh headed for Mr. Wicker's, taking the birthday card with him.

Large soot-colored clouds hung low, and halfway to the house an icy drizzle fell. Josh ran the rest of the way.

Mr. Wicker was surprised by Josh's visit, and he said so.

"I really came to see Matthew," said Josh.

A troubled look clouded Mr. Wicker's eyes. "I don't see too much of him; he spends so much time in the tunnel. I feel as if I've let him down." Then Mr. Wicker asked Josh why he wanted to see Matthew.

Josh rubbed his hand across his head, shaking out the wetness. "Well, you see, today is my birthday, and I thought I'd share it with Matthew. He told me that he's never had one."

"That's true," said Mr. Wicker. "Oh dear," he exclaimed. "Had I known it was your birthday I would have had a cake for you."

"Oh, that's all right," said Josh.

"If you don't mind a ready-mix birthday cake I can get one going in a hurry," said Mr. Wicker.

"It's all right with me," said Josh. He went to the fireplace cupboard and called Matthew. Minutes passed before the door opened, and when it did, it opened very slowly.

Matthew appeared with his hands behind his back. "Happy birthday, Josh," he said, and he handed Josh a card that he had made himself.

"Thank you," said Josh. "Happy birthday to you!" He gave Matthew the card he had made.

"For me?" said Matthew, surprised.

"Yes, from now on your birthday is the same as mine," said Josh.

"How come?" said Matthew, bewildered.

"It's very simple," said Josh. "Since today is my birthday, I'm going to give away part of it to you." He smiled.

Matthew continued to look confused; then he shrugged his shoulders and said, "Well okay, if it's all right with you."

The smell of a cake baking drifted across the kitchen.

"I even have birthday candles to put on the cake," said Mr. Wicker. He wrote across the cake with chocolate: HAPPY BIRTHDAY JOSH AND MATTHEW.

"Remember, you must make a wish before you blow out the candles," said Mr. Wicker. "Wish hard—birthday wishes count."

Josh and Matthew closed their eyes to wish. Daphne jumped up on the table to sniff at the cake, and Mr. Wicker pulled her away, saying, "It's not your birthday, Daphne; it's theirs."

They blew all the candles out and sang "Happy Birthday" to each other. Mr. Wicker's eyes got watery.

Mr. Wicker and Josh gave their attention to Matthew, who seemed happier than he'd been in a long time.

Josh returned to Cragsmoor whistling "Happy Birthday."

After history class one day, Mr. Wicker called Josh aside. "I've something important to tell you," he said. Josh could sense the excitement in his voice. "I think Matthew has gone to wherever he had to go to in the first place," Mr. Wicker said. "I guess what I'm trying to say is that I don't think Matthew is a ghost any longer."

"That's great," cried Josh. "I wish we could have said good-bye."

"The strangest thing happened," said Mr. Wicker. "Must be a coincidence though. When Matthew disappeared, I discovered the whirligig gone."

"That is funny," said Josh. "Who do you think took it?"

"Obviously someone who liked it a lot," answered the old teacher.

Huge ice floes jammed the river. Josh stood alone on the bank tossing snowballs onto them. Matthew's sudden disappearance made Josh wonder if his birthday wish for him had come true, or maybe it was what Matthew had wished for himself. Then Josh thought that perhaps the birthday celebration was enough to send Matthew to where he had to go.

In the weeks that followed at Cragsmoor, Josh made the tennis team because of Miles' coaching. He told Josh that he would like him to come home with him at Eastertime and try out the courts at his house. Josh liked the idea of spending Easter with Miles, and he decided that from then on he was going to make his own plans. He wrote and told his mother not to worry about him at Easter.

Mr. Wicker announced his retirement. He was moving to St. Petersburg, Florida. On the day he left, Josh went to his house to say good-bye.

The house looked friendless, like a bird's nest in winter. Inside, the rooms were bare. A wind swept through the fireplace, scattering cold ashes. Mr. Wicker stood in the kitchen with Daphne in his arms and a small box at his feet.

"Everything's gone," said Josh.

"Yes it is," said Mr. Wicker, looking around the room. He sighed. "I was a young man when I first came here to live and teach at Cragsmoor. It was a long time ago—but now that I'm leaving, it all seems to have gone by so quickly."

Josh stroked Daphne. "Good-bye," he said. He fought back tears.

Mr. Wicker placed his hand on Josh's shoulder. "I buried Oliver on top of the hill, not too far from Matthew."

"I'm glad they're near each other," said Josh. "We never did find out how Matthew died."

"That's not important, Josh," said Mr. Wicker. "It's how we live that matters." He smiled.

Josh watched from the bridge as Otis Wicker drove away slowly in his old car. As Josh stood there, he thought he heard a whistling sound. He looked at the smokehouse roof but the whirligig was gone.

The crow appeared from under the eaves, flew to the top of the hill, and came to rest on a branch. He cawed loudly. The snow was beginning to melt, and Josh wondered what the daffodils would look like on the hill.

5